Almighty Matters

Almighty Matters

God's Hidden Politics in the Bible

Nicholas Berry

RESOURCE *Publications* • Eugene, Oregon

ALMIGHTY MATTERS
God's Hidden Politics in the Bible

Copyright © 2015 Nicholas Berry. All rights reserved. Except for brief quotations in critical publications or reviews, no part of this book may be reproduced in any manner without prior written permission from the publisher. Write: Permissions. Wipf and Stock Publishers, 199 W. 8th Ave., Suite 3, Eugene, OR 97401.

Resource Publications
An Imprint of Wipf and Stock Publishers
199 W. 8th Ave., Suite 3
Eugene, OR 97401

www.wipfandstock.com

ISBN 13: 978-1-4982-3421-4

Manufactured in the U.S.A.   12/23/2015

Including more than 500 verse citations would require a letter of permission from the publisher below. *Almighty Matters* quotes only 284 verses.

Revised Standard Version of the Bible, copyright 1952 [2nd edition, 1971] by the Division of Christian Education of the National Council of Churches of Christ in the United States of America. Used by permission. All rights reserved.

Contents

Foreword | vii
Preface | xi
Acknowledgments | xvii

Part I—The Hebrew Bible | 1

1. Creation: Who Has the Power? | 3
2. The People of Genesis: A Blessed Human Nature | 14
3. God as Realtor: One Land, Two Peoples | 28
4. Moses: A Template for Political Leadership | 36
5. War and State Creation | 57
6. Political Power: Glory, Corruption, and Collapse | 65

Part II—The Christian Bible | 79

7. Jesus the Politician | 85
8. The Subversion of Rome | 106
9. The Politics of Death and Resurrection | 122
10. Epilogue: Unanswered Questions | 125

Bibliography | 135

Foreword

THE IDEA FOR THIS book had its beginning in 1961 on the island of Malta, then a British colony. I was on a six-month deployment on a Navy minesweeper as part of the Sixth Fleet. We enjoyed various liberty ports. As a general rule, I would read up on the history of the places that we would dock. For Malta, this included learning about its occupiers and all the famous battles fought for control of this strategic Mediterranean island. I remembered that St. Paul was shipwrecked here and had converted many to Christianity.

I was the officer in charge of a diving team. We were called frogmen then, two varieties. We were EOD (Explosive Ordnance Disposal); others, more gung ho, were UDT (Underwater Demolition Team). By chance, a UDT group arrived for liberty in the capital (Valletta) at the same time we did. By chance again, I met them in a pub, and they invited me to join them in a dive for fun. They picked the entrance to St. Paul's Bay. We found it barely thirty yards wide, as I remember it, with vertical rocky cliffs sandwiching the entrance. We anchored our diving boat outside the inlet in about eighty feet of rough water. No wonder that ships under sail have had difficulty transiting the narrow entrance into the bay, including the one carrying St. Paul on his way to Rome. It crashed on the bottom and sank. Fortunately, Paul could swim or cling onto the wreckage. He managed to make it into the bay safely.

Foreword

We put on our tanks and headed down to the bottom at the bay's entrance. There we found the knurled wooden ribs of an ancient vessel sticking out of the sand. The planking was long gone and the ribs showed substantial deterioration.

Remember, this was 1961, less than a decade after the aqualung opened up extensive scuba diving anywhere. We were likely the first divers to explore the area. As proof, less than a month later my diving team discovered an ancient harbor where Roman ships could shelter to avoid heavy weather off the coast of Sardinia. The bottom, at 128 feet, was littered with amphora—those two-handled, big ceramic jars that Greeks and Romans used to transport wine, olive oil, and water. Clearly, no one had preceded us, or these valuable antiques would have been harvested.

And the dive at Malta was dangerous, with the current surging even on the bottom.

Afterwards, I decided that our discovery, which could be the remains of the very ship that carried Paul, needed to be announced and explored.

The next day I went to the national museum in Valletta, having already met the curator on a previous visit. He was busy but spared me a moment. "What is known about the wreck at the entrance to St. Paul's Bay?" I asked. "I dove there yesterday."

"What wreck?" he replied and then turned away and left to deal with one of his staff members.

Stunned, I just stood there. He apparently had no interest in my claim. With our ship's departure imminent, I dropped the issue, and have often wondered since then whether any archeological efforts have been made to explore and analyze the wreck. It very well could be that shifting sands have long covered the remains or that storms have further dismantled it.

So began my very long exploration of the Bible as history and politics.

Luke, in his "Acts of the Apostles," writes of Paul's wreck and his time on Malta. I read it that night. Somehow a seed was planted. It sprouted a few weeks later in Rome. Because I was not part of the minesweeper's company, when we hit port I was gone

Foreword

for the duration of the stay. My guidebook listed all the sites where Christianity and the Roman Empire had mixed. The Coliseum, the catacombs, the Arch of Titus showing in relief the spoils from the sack of Jerusalem, and St. Peter's in the Vatican made the list. I read their stories.

In the years just before this experience and for all years since, I have been a churchgoer, a believer. Some may wonder what the content of that belief could be. My wife, Janet, and I were married as Methodists and stayed so in Pittsburgh, where I studied for my PhD in politics; shifted to become Episcopalians when teaching at Lynchburg College, then to Presbyterians when at Cornell College in Iowa, then to Lutherans when at Ursinus College in Pennsylvania; and, finally, a return to Episcopalians when on a Fulbright Lectureship in New Zealand, at a defense think tank in Washington, and now as a writer in Annapolis, Maryland.

This circuitous Christianity compelled me to explore doctrine, the Bible, and church history. Of course, I did it with the eyes and mind of a political scientist, questioning everything that could be questioned. This learning process naturally seeped into my profession. For years I taught courses titled: "World Leaders," "Political Leadership," and "War and Revolution." Without much design, the leadership of Moses; the brilliant military strategies of Joshua; the establishment of empires, including that of Rome; and the struggle of Christians in that empire became class topics, with appropriate readings. There is an obvious and substantial political history in the Bible.

The study of Middle East politics also came naturally. I was a month-long guest of the Gaddafi regime as the teacher on Libyan history for a group of visiting American and Canadian Muslims in 1981; interviewed Palestinian leaders in Egypt and Jordan in 1996; dined with a well-known Israeli professor in Netanya, Israel, on the same trip; chatted informally with former prime minister Ehud Barak at the World Economic Forum in Davos, Switzerland, in 2005; and broke a number of stories about the Arab-Israeli conflict in newspapers here and abroad. I am co-author of an international relations textbook now in its ninth edition and write the Middle East chapters.

I have retired after four terms as Democratic Party chairman here in Annapolis, opening a vast space of time. Although I remain Director of Foreign Policy Forum, a Web site, as well as a columnist in *The Capital*, our local newspaper, they still leave space.

The Bible as a template for politics became my original theme for the book, the first inspiration. Many biblical lessons have guided more modern politics dealing with creation, human nature, nation- and state-building, war, leadership, slavery, feminism, foreign occupations, and subversion. Politicians have actually emulated the actions of biblical characters. In addition, since many biblical stories from the Hebrew and Christian Bibles have entered a global culture, their lessons have become part of habitual politics.

While still referred to in the book, this theme is now somewhat minor, perhaps because it is so obvious to anyone familiar with the Bible that little new material would warrant a book. I needed a new approach, something new to write.

The case I will make is this: The Hebrew and Christian Bibles are politically connected. What Christians call the New Testament is a virtual extension of the politics of the Old. To miss their underlying politics is to fail to grasp Christian theology.

Many readers will find this theme outrageous; all should find it new.

Preface

ALMIGHTY MATTERS: GOD'S HIDDEN POLITICS IN THE BIBLE is an examination of politics in the Bible, a juxtaposition of topics that may strike some readers as surprising. After all, most people—especially believers—view the Bible as the primary source of spiritual insight, ethical wisdom, and moral guidance. The association of this holy book with the world of politics, which many consider inherently corrupt and self-serving—or at least morally compromised—might appear unseemly.

But this view shuts out a major, if not the most prominent, theme of the Bible. This theme reveals a hidden political progression linking the Hebrew Bible with the Christian. Biblical history begins with an account of the origins, development, and establishment of the Hebrew state, and its ultimate political failure. This failure establishes the link with the Christian Bible, which is the history of correcting that failure with a new political strategy.

Religion drives politics in the Hebrew Bible in the sense that the religious beliefs of the Hebrews shape their political activities. The Bible presents God and his agents working together, freeing his chosen people from captivity; turning them into a nation; bolstering them with supportive myths; assigning them a land of their own; providing laws, ceremonies, and customs; hardening them with lengthy wanderings in the wilderness; honing their military skills;

appointing judges; and helping them fight their way into the Promised Land, where they establish a state. All this is standard politics. What is unique is the perceived role of God and his commands.

The Israelites build a mighty capital and militarily expand their domain. Their leaders confidently expand their governing authority. God is less present. Mighty empires confront them. They are defeated, occupied, taken off into captivity, restored, occupied again and again, and headed for destruction and diaspora.

This is political failure of the first order.

From a very promising beginning, it is all downhill from then on. Political incompetence weakens the polity. The prophets blame the Israelites for turning away from God as the cause of their political troubles, especially for the Babylonian conquest and exile. They see unlawful intermarriages, the failure to follow prescribed ceremonies, and disobedience to God's voice.

The prophets are wrong, or at least they fail to portray the complete picture. They see the conquest through the lens of a purely religious perspective, missing a practical political reason. That conquest and those that follow—Persian, Greek, and Roman—have little to do with sin. The Jews are done in by their reliance on their military culture, their neglect of diplomacy, devastating conflicts between Israel and Judah, and their religious structures that biologically restrict the size of their nation. In an era of large warrior empires, the numbers-limited Jews are doomed. They don't understand that their militant political-religious culture condemns their state.

In contrast, politics drives religion in the Christian Bible in the sense that the creation of Christianity is the fulfillment of Jesus' politics. Jesus sets out to correct the political failure of his people.

His political strategy to redeem his people and to expand God's people has two mutually reinforcing prongs, although each is capable of standing on its own. The first, and apparently dominant, strategy is to publicize an apocalyptic event, where God and the Son of man will soon come and destroy evil and those who represent it, including Rome. In this new peaceable kingdom of God, Jesus will rule. In support of the apocalypse, the second

Preface

prong has Jesus' apostles proselytize the Jews and the Gentiles—the mass of common people—with his gospel message of salvation. They, especially Paul, spread the word throughout the Roman Empire. This political-religious movement, founded by Jesus, creates Christianity. Its members are to be on the right side when the apocalypse occurs.

Alas, the apocalypse does not happen. Jesus somehow misreads God's intentions or, rather, uses them in his own way.

Nevertheless, it is the second prong of his strategy that does the job. Jesus' political strategy is to work from the bottom up, recruiting the masses—not only Jews but Gentiles as well. Jesus invents politics for the powerless. He lays the foundation for the subversion of the Roman Empire. God's now-expanded people need to be under the protection of a larger government—one that they capture. God's people will then have proper political protection and a vehicle for creating even more of God's people.

This is the first, or clearly one of the first, historical records of a mass political movement growing to the point that it captures the state. Of course, the Roman state adopts the Christian movement—a marriage of church and state—exactly as Jesus intended. The concept of the separation of church and state did not yet exist; thus, to create a big, popular religion inevitably creates the requirement that it have its own state. Christianity would not have been possible without the Roman Empire. It will also be noted that the Roman Empire (Byzantium) would not have lasted over 1,000 more years without Christianity.

The Epilogue (chapter 10) considers some additional questions.

Does the book analyze the issue of the Bible's historical accuracy? I take both of the Bibles at face value, dealing with accepted events and knowing that historians raise numerous questions about the reliability of particulars.

Does the emergence of ever-prominent human free will in biblical stories indicate that God is losing command of history? We argue that people take more and more authority and why this is inevitable.

Preface

Are the Jews still God's chosen people? We make the case that they are. The failed Jewish revolt of 66–70 CE and the one that follows it (nothing seems to have been learned in Jerusalem about politics) creates the Jewish diaspora. Here the Jews perform a great service to the world. More than any other peoples, they enrich what has become the world's dominant culture. Monotheism and a culture poetically, ethically, musically, economically, historically, scientifically, architecturally, and artistically advanced is a contribution by the Jews that has no equal. In short, Jews believe that they are God's chosen people and act accordingly. This is the cement of historical Jewish unity and their great cultural mission and impulse to return to the Promised Land. Additionally, orthodox Christianity and Islam accept Jews as people of the book—the same God for all—and consider Jews to be a true expression of his will. Christians, it should be noted, also play a key role in the re-establishment of modern Israel.

Were all these political events ordained by God, were they the product of historical necessity, or were they just happenstance? This is delicate territory. God could be seen as confessing that he had made a mistake by limiting his chosen people to biological Jews and so condemning them to occupation and persecution. He needs Jesus to bail him out. And does Jesus actually reject his Judaism? I will argue that both suppositions above are false. Still, my thesis will raise controversy.

I have long studied the Bible, curious after finding what I thought could be the wreck of St. Paul's ship at the bottom of the entrance to St. Paul's Bay in Malta. I was a Navy frogman, as we were called then, over fifty years ago. Paul's story began the quest. As noted in the *Foreword*, the more I studied, the more it became apparent to me that the Bible is rich in politics and history. In over thirty years of college teaching, I frequently used the Bible in class to analyze political leadership, military strategy, nationalism, state creation, and philosophy. A confession: It has taken me all these years to discover—yes, that is the right word—the pattern of the Bible's politics described above. It's been a singular enterprise, for

Preface

I have yet to discover the theses organizing this book from any source. Once it came to me, this project became an obsession.

As a political science professor; former two-term mayor; political party chair in two cities; and author of six books, many articles in journals, and hundreds of newspaper columns, I discern and analyze politics. Much of my writing is about the Middle East.

Acknowledgments

I HAD NO IDEA after graduating from college that my working years would heavily involve writing as a columnist, defense analyst, textbook and monograph author, and Web site director. So was it sheer luck or destiny that I married a summa cum laude English major? Janet has many virtues and talents (she is an accomplished actress), including the ability to flag my improper grammar and tangled sentences. She is my live-in editor.

Others also shaped what writing talent I have into something better. Professor E.E. Roberts at Bethany College (West Virginia), my alma mater; Col. Dan Smith, director of research at Washington's Center for Defense Information, where I worked after retiring from college teaching; and Lynn Berry (our daughter), at this writing the news editor for the Associated Press in Moscow, Russia, all insisted that I write clearly and properly and worked diligently to help me do so.

As the idea for this book took form, Karl Weber, my consulting editor, kept badgering me to sharpen my overall theme. Unconnected political musings about the Bible would not do. He saw that a new political story line could emerge from my scattered biblical commentary and asked me to develop one. For that I am grateful. As the cliché goes, Weber made me see the forest and not just the trees.

Acknowledgments

Dr. Christopher Dreisbach, Director of Applied Ethics and Humanities at Johns Hopkins University and Professor of Moral and Systematic Theology at the Ecumenical Institute of Theology, St. Mary's Seminary and University, and a new friend; and Dr. David Weddle, Professor of Religion Emeritus at Colorado College, an old colleague, gave helpful and critical appraisals of the book during the writing. The Rev. Dr. Amy Richter, rector at St. Anne's Episcopal Church in Annapolis, Maryland, and her husband and assistant rector, Joe Pagano, gave their encouragement and a platform in their Sunday Forum for me to discuss the book's theme. I am indebted to them for all their suggestions and support.

Two friends, Therese Bouchard, an activist and writer on mental health, and Sarah Flynn, a consulting editor who has worked with a number of well-known authors, have helped explain the publishing business beyond my knowledge and experience.

For making me aware of Wipf and Stock publishers, I have Warren and Marilyn Hollinshead and Preston Kavanagh to thank. Preston, who has had three of his books published by Wipf and Stock, also introduced me to Barbara Oldroyd, a superb copyeditor. Barbara put the manuscript into the proper format for the publisher and, more importantly, flagged things that my wife, Janet, had missed.

Finally, but essentially, Matthew Wimer, the editor at Wipf and Stock, skillfully worked with me to manage the details of putting *Almighty Matters* into print, and James Stock, its Marketing Director, helped develop a plan to market the book, making the most of my enthusiastic efforts to connect the book with a variety of potential readers.

Part I

The Hebrew Bible

THIS IS THE STORY of God and his agents creating a religion among a biologically related group of people. They then create a political state. The government of this chosen people is located in a land assigned by God. God and those who speak in his name direct the politics of the Israelites. In this ancient world, where there is religion there must be a government, and where there is a government there must be a religion. There is no separation of religion (church) and government (state). They are one. Thus, the establishment of the Hebrew religion has to aim at the establishment of a political state. We begin our political analysis with the Torah—the Five Books of Moses: Genesis, Exodus, Leviticus, Numbers, and Deuteronomy. The political history continues from First Samuel through Ezra. From patriarchal origins, through bondage in Egypt, to wanderings and conquest of the Promised Land, the Israelites prosper. Alas, Hebrew history does not end well—divisions, defeats, occupation, exile, more occupations, and their state extinguished. Corrupt and incompetent political leaders, not God, are to blame.

The reader must note that the Hebrew and Christian Bibles will be treated at face value. Both theologians and historians have agreed that there are clear contradictions, discrepancies, and

Part I—The Hebrew Bible

chronological errors in them. They will not intrude here. We will look for common political themes, events, and facts in an analysis that does not depend on questionable biblical statements. Thus, it is not necessary to treat every word in the Bibles as a God-given fact. It is, however, necessary to treat the Bibles as genuine portrayals of the historical course of two religions and of two very different politics.

— CHAPTER 1 —

Creation: Who Has the Power?

As the cliché goes, let us begin at the beginning.

Actually, God must be present before the beginning. God must know who he is—what capabilities he has as God. The Hebrew Bible illustrates these capabilities, which have many facets or aspects.

The first aspect is somewhat obvious. He has the ability to do great things, creating great things both in nature and in shaping his subjects' behavior. In short, he has power. A god that has no power cannot be God. He—gods tend to be males, although goddesses also exist—must be able to have a decisive impact on history. A god that cannot do anything, command anything, or plan anything is no god at all. God's power, therefore, comes from no one else or no other source. His will is the source of his power. He can create anything that he contemplates.

Second, God can make others believe that he is God. Having a God presumes that there are others who are *not* God—those who are prospective followers and believers. And if these others do not believe that God is God, what is the point of being a god? Where is the power? Nowhere. The others will have no idea about the source of the things that they experience. Worse, they will attribute to something or somebody else what God has done.

Part I—The Hebrew Bible

God will acquire followers. To get others to believe in him, God will speak to them, telling them of him and his power. They will listen, of course. But what would make them listen?

Well, God will back up his words with proof. God will demonstrate that when he tells them that he will do X, X happens. They will witness X. Words and compatible actions are potent proof that he exists and has great capabilities.

But God will not do everything by himself, because to do so will diminish his power. The others, his followers, without any power are mere playthings. They don't have to think about anything or do anything. Most importantly, they don't have to honor God. Worse, they have no choice in obeying God or not. God would be in total control. God's followers need some measure of free will. To be seen as a great God, he needs for them to choose him, celebrate him, and do his will with their will. And God will find helpers.

God will recruit agents—leaders who will follow him and get others to do the same. As long as the believers have a will of their own, that will is to be shaped and maintained in God's favor. Although God can do everything himself, that is no challenge. And it is a lot of work. Others need to help. Being God is an ongoing process, not a one-shot affair.

This means that God will give followers rules to live by. God has standards and others have to abide by them. They need help, and providing rules for them will certainly help them become God's people. Yes, those who follow God are, by definition, God's people. Now rules are all well and good, but rules aren't worth much if there are no rewards for following them or punishments for disobedience. For this reason, God fashions rules so that they bring benefits if followed and costs if not. Furthermore, the more people who follow God and his rules, the better. This will marginalize other so-called gods, making God supreme. God's team is the biggest, the most powerful. This power, more than anything, validates God as God.

One can only conclude that God in the Hebrew Bible fits the bill. This is good news for the Hebrews.

Creation: Who Has the Power?

Power is a key concept in the realm of politics.

The Hebrew founding fathers fashion a creation story that endows the people chosen by that all-powerful creator as embodying, representing, and employing the creator's power. They publicize, eventually in the Hebrew Bible, what they hear God tell them—that he created heaven and earth. Believing that God created the heaven and earth and all that dwells upon it compels believers to conclude that God owns what he has created and has authority over its residents. Their rent, as occupiers of God's creation, is their devotion and obedience to the Almighty. Not being a theologian, I can clearly understand that this set of beliefs becomes the foundation for God's covenant with his people and why creation is a central belief in the three Abrahamic religions. As Professor Michael Walzer expresses in his book, "God was Israel's king; Israel was God's vassal or servant nation."[1]

The key point in our story is this: The Hebrew Bible relates the history of a people who firmly believe God commands that they establish a religious state. They must rule themselves. Rule by an alien means that that ruler has another god or gods and will enforce wrongful worship. Political and religious unity is mandatory. And with God on their side, these people are bound to be politically spectacular and ever successful.

There is a flaw in this logic, however, as I will analyze when reviewing the collapse of the Jewish state, but the belief that their God is the powerful creator and helper sets the stage for the entire Hebrew history. It also sets the stage for the necessity for God via Jesus to create a Christian state by subverting and capturing the Roman Empire.

The connection between power and politics is intimate. Politics includes all the activities and ideas for and about leading a group. The components of politics are numerous: defining group membership, establishing the rules for selecting leaders and making laws and policies, providing law enforcement, adjudicating disputes, providing services to the group, conducting ceremonies, creating symbols, defending the group, and working with other

---

1. Walzer, *In God's Shadow: Politics in the Hebrew Bible*, 6.

groups. These activities and ideas associated with them all require power, with power defined as the capacity to gain compliance. Groups and group leaders need it to create all the political components listed above. For example, groups need a process to select leaders, which must be (or at least should be) complied with, and the leaders selected need group members to comply with duly created laws and judicial decisions. Anarchy—life without governing power—is like a vacuum that nature abhors. Without political order, as Thomas Hobbes writes in *Leviathan*, life will be poor, nasty, brutish, and short—a war of all against all. This means that the leader or leaders of a group must have supreme power. There cannot be two sovereign (supreme controlling) governments for one people. If there are, then who are the people to obey? Won't the two governments struggle to gain supreme power? And that will create a Hobbesian state, with all of life's attendant problems.

There are many ways to exercise power: physical force, intimidation, enculturation, persuasion, and social pressure; the Bible, as we will examine, illustrates all of them. Life for humans, whose social nature is mandatory, cannot exist without the reality of power—and thus without politics.

Religion is designed to be a unifying force in politics, but inevitably results in being a divisive force in politics as well if there are disputes about religion within a religion or between competing religions. As I have noted above, a set of religious beliefs designates who represents God's power. This means that competing religious beliefs inevitably produce more than one belief regarding who should have power, especially in an era before the strictures separating church and state. As Hobbes notes, competing sources of power raise the question of who is in charge of the group. Disobeying the competing source of power, as noted, brings social disorder. The resulting conflict has costs related to security, welfare, and economic production. As we trace the history of the Hebrews, their push for religious unity seeks political unity and all the benefits that come from social order. Alas, there will be religious disunity at times, with all the ills that it brings.

Creation: Who Has the Power?

Religion and politics rarely mix calmly, whether within a group or between groups. A strong case can be made that the origin of the problem lies with the creation story in Genesis. Power is the central issue here as well. Those who are not the chosen people have power, too, embodying, they believe, the same willpower that the chosen possess. The Hebrew Bible is filled with conflicts between the Hebrews and others.

Similar conflicts rage today.

The prime issue is still the source of power. Today's conflicts further illustrate the connection between religion and politics, and the United States is no exception.

Creationists take Genesis as history, giving God and those who say they speak on his behalf the edge in legitimate political power. Evolutionists treat the allegorical creation story as validating God and defining human nature (see chapter 2). They see science at work, making humans more in control of life in terms of knowledge and politics.

Whichever side wins out has a huge effect on politics. The winners, who then control government, whether religious or secular, produce different policies over issues of law, morality, education, police, and political compromise to the detriment of the losers.

Creationists take as fact that God created everything: the universe, the planets and stars, land and water, plants and animals, and, most importantly, human beings, both male and female. They also believe that God directs humans, tells them what to do and not do, and even appoints his elect to rule according to his instructions. In short, there is a connection between these ideas and the idea that those who speak for God should have control of political power.

The Hebrews are creationists, of course.

By portraying God, their God, as the maker of heaven and earth and all that dwells therein, the Hebrews have created a founding myth that makes them very special people. In effect, they are God's chosen. This myth is self-serving, of course, but most, if not all, myths are self-serving to those who harbor them. God, this all-powerful being, favors them. His power is their gift. This gives their nation great potential, because of the power behind it.

Part I—The Hebrew Bible

The Hebrews are thereby endowed with great confidence to carry out God's plan, prevailing over other people and their rulers. No thought can be given to accepting alien rule. That would be an affront to God. Such a belief in one's God, a congenial idea, motivates Moses, Aaron, and the tribal leaders as they, following God's commands, decide to leave captivity in Egypt. It sustains them through their arduous wandering and maturing as a nation. Starting a nation from scratch and building it to historical greatness requires great hope, and the creation story provides it.

Those who see the creation story as allegory may still see God as a creator but not God or his agents as their rightful secular ruler. Secular Roman Catholics, Episcopalians, and other so-called mainline denominations, as well as Conservative and Reformist Jews, fit this category. As an Episcopalian, I see every Sunday my evolution-believing fellow parishioners repeating the creationist Nicene Creed without a thought of noting any implications for maintaining their secular beliefs.

Even evolutionist politicians are tempted to put God on their side. Like the Hebrews, doing so elevates their people. The United States is a prime example—perhaps the most blatant evolutionist practitioner of the Lordly marriage of God and state. The Pledge of Allegiance of the United States places the country "under God." The country's money proclaims "In God We Trust." Americans sing "God Bless America" on the assumption that he does.

A close cousin of creationism is the notion of "intelligent design." Although these folks agree that the scientific evidence for evolution is overwhelming, they believe that God guides the process. It is, of course, a conclusion based on faith, not historical evidence. In court battles (the political implications of religion inevitably reach the American judicial system), secularists treat those who favor intelligent design as fronts for creationists.

The cases usually involve prayer and Bible reading in public schools, the display of religious symbols on public lands, and issues that I will note later in this chapter. In the prohibition contained in the First Amendment to the United States—"Congress shall make no law respecting the establishment of religion or the free exercise

Creation: Who Has the Power?

thereof"—the Supreme Court has interpreted "Congress" as being the equivalent of any government body. These cases (some of which will be noted at the end of this chapter) affirm the close, often contentious, relationship between religion and politics.

At the conclusion of the chapter, we will further illustrate this divide in current politics. But first, let's revisit the creation in Genesis.

Right away there is a problem.

The author of Genesis writes that God created light on the first day, producing day and night, but the sun and moon were only created on the fourth day. Maybe, however, this sequence portends a great insight. The light that God created could be interpreted as the Big Bang, creating a new day of all existence. Certainly the release of so much energy sufficient to establish a universe must have produced a lot of light.

As one of the clergy at my church told me: "Who do you think set off the Big Bang?"

If that is true, God existed before time, because time began only with the Big Bang (as explained in *A Brief History of Time* by Stephen Hawking). That would make God many billions of years old. Even if only a spirit, God had to be the spirit of something. But for many people, as my church clergyman said, God has always been, without being created.

Well, this is a mystery. In many religions other than the Abrahamic ones of Judaism, Christianity, and Islam, God emerges from pre-existing humans. With God a spirit of those humans, this would make the spirit arise only with the advent of the human species. Why couldn't God be the spirit of the first human—an Adam, if you will? There is a problem with that, because Genesis tells us that God created Adam.

Maybe there is a simpler explanation.

Many religions have a creation story. They begin there. To make their god or gods genuine and true, what better way than to have them be the number one power. If the ability to create heaven and earth and all living creatures is not the franchise of number one, nothing is. All things have a creation, after all, and the

Part I—The Hebrew Bible

universe is no exception. Someone (or something with the natural forces of evolution filling that role) had to be the creator. The vast majority of Christians, Jews, and probably Muslims believe in evolution and God. For some, God guided evolution. For others, God is a product of evolution, part of the human and spiritual experience. He did, according to Genesis, make man in his own image (Gen 1:26–27). Furthermore, God said to male and female to "fill the earth and subdue it; and have dominion over the fish of the sea and over the birds of the air and over every living thing that moves upon the earth. And God said, 'Behold, I have given you every plant yielding seed which is upon the face of all the earth, and to every bird of the air, and to everything that creeps on the earth, and everything that has the breath of life'" (Gen 1:28–30).

Well, not everything, as we will see with Adam and Eve eating what is forbidden.

At first blush, God is making humans the top animal, with dominion over just about everything. This can be interpreted as humans having free will and being in control. However, this is very soon contradicted, when God orders Adam and Eve to leave the Garden of Eden.

This is a puzzle.

There are many puzzles in the Hebrew and Christian Bibles. Disputes over biblical interpretation have corralled political authorities to weigh in on one side or the other. The Reformation challenge to the Roman Catholic Church—mainly over structure, scripture, and church doctrine—spawned Europe's first worst war. Politicians invariably settle disputes that rock social stability and their rule, and religion has been a great source of social instability. To head off these disputes, some political rulers have mandated that they are the protectors of a religion, are rulers in its name and scriptures, and brook no opposition, including in their use of force. As such, religion so captured becomes the basis of dictatorship, or at least some heavy authoritarianism.

America's Founding Fathers authored the First Amendment—"Congress shall make no law respecting the establishment of religion or the free exercise thereof . . ."—precisely to avoid this

Creation: Who Has the Power?

outcome. It goes without saying that this did not eliminate disputes over its implementation. Current conflicts over such issues as the display of religious symbols on public property, gay marriage, evolution, abortion, and contraception divide Americans politically.

One further note on creation has political import. After the sixth day of creation—time in the Bible is often a flexible phenomenon—God takes note of his creation and "behold, it was very good" (Gen 1:31). Environmentalists take this as God's first political advice. If all that is created in Genesis is good, then humans and their governments seem to have a clear obligation to keep it that way. Unfortunately, other political factions favor the reckless exploitation of natural resources.

We will see in later chapters that the Bible is a rich source of political policy advice—the good, the bad, and the antiquated.

So, is the creation story in Genesis history or an allegory? Catholics, Episcopalians, and other denominations use the Nicene Creed (presented later, in chapter 7) as the basis of their faith, and it is explicitly creationist. A tradition that is eighteen centuries old is hard to discard.

The reader may be wondering: So what? What harm is there in believing that God is the creator of the universe and all that is in it?

Good question.

Faith fills the gap with what is not provable. Answers are given to mystery and, to bolster a religion, making up an answer may be necessary. For some, this makes religion a product of human imagination, satisfying the need to explain what is unexplainable. For others, questions of creation and other mysteries produce answers that must be true given their faith. So an omnipotent God had to have the power to create everything.

Politics, as noted at the beginning of the chapter, deals fundamentally with power. Defined as the capacity to achieve purposeful results, power is involved in attaining the leadership role in a group, maintaining that role, producing laws and policies, gaining compliance with these laws and policies, and managing relations with other groups and their leaders.

Part I—The Hebrew Bible

The Genesis story is, among other things, a story about who has power. As we shall explore in chapter 2, a struggle—if that is the right word—between humans and God as to who will make history begins there. Who has power? This theme is prominently embedded in both the Hebrew and Christian Bibles. For many, including Muslims and those of other faiths, it is still a live question today. Two cases illustrate this point.

The Scopes Trial, sarcastically also called the Scopes Monkey Trial, became famous in 1925. John Scopes, a Tennessee high school teacher, was charged by state authorities with violating a state law that banned the teaching of evolution. The Democratic Party, which was then in power there (descendants are now mostly Republicans), attached itself to fundamentalist Christianity, the dominant position of most Tennesseans, in order to maintain its power base. It even brought in three-time presidential candidate William Jennings Bryan to assist in the prosecution. Renowned trial lawyer Clarence Darrow volunteered to defend Scopes. It took the jury nine minutes to arrive at a guilty verdict. As evidence of its political nature, in 1968, the United States Supreme Court ruled in Eppserson v. Arkansas that such bans violated the Establishment Clause of the First Amendment.

The second case—the Texas battle over whether to teach creationism/intelligent design along with evolution in public schools—has been before the State Board of Education for years. The issue is whether they should be included in public school textbooks—especially intelligent design, which, in its extreme form, specifies that an unnamed entity, not evolution, created animals and humans. In February 2014, the Board, clearly seeking to defuse the issue, decided to give priority over textbook review panels to teachers and professors, rather than politically oriented advocates of the near-creationist proposition.

Both cases hinge on bolstering the political power of those who say that they speak in God's name following God's word versus those who speak for what they say science and reason have concluded. Many in the latter group willfully state that science and reason are God's gift, part of the dominion in creation.

Creation: Who Has the Power?

In fact, there is a very long history of political rulers using religion to legitimate and guide their rule, from the time of Moses; through Christian kings, Muslim caliphs, and colonial American governors; to today's Israel and Iran. Islamic terrorists take it to extremes, as did the far earlier Christian Crusaders.

The mix of politics and religion has not often been a happy one. Power is the issue.

We will see in the Bible that in the beginning God has enormous power to control things, whereas humans have very little. But humans start the process to take more power for themselves. God lets them take it, or, as some would say, cannot prevent their doing so. One interpretation could be that God helps humans become more capable of controlling their own destiny and, as they mature, humans naturally take more power. Human experience and science then accelerate human notions that they control history, and if bad things happen then humans are at fault, not God. God's job then is to love, comfort, inspire, and guide individual humans in coping with life.

So let's look at how the relationship between humans and God begins. Besides questions of political power, concepts of human nature are revealed that shape and are the foundations of political philosophy.

The stories in Genesis portraying Adam, Eve, Cain, Abel, Noah, Abraham, Isaac, and Ishmael continue to reveal the nature of God, humans, and their relationships. Power, and thus politics, is front and center.

CHAPTER 2

The People of Genesis: A Blessed Human Nature

THE CREATION STORY, INCLUDING the introduction of man and woman, although not history as such, is a powerful commentary on the nature of the relations between God and humans. Questions of political power are clearly evident and, as we will explore later in the chapter, concepts of human nature shape, even determine, political philosophy. And adherence to a political philosophy largely shapes political behavior. Thus, God's task is clear. He must instill a concept of human nature in his people, thereby creating a political philosophy that will produce the necessary behavior to carry out God's intentions of creating and organizing his chosen people and establishing their own government on a designated land.

According to Genesis, God creates man on the sixth day. Again, man and later woman come last in the creation story, exactly as evolution would posit.

What is really important is that God, on the sixth day, gives man "dominion over the fish of the sea, over the birds of the air, and over the cattle, and over all the earth, and over every creeping thing that creeps upon the earth" (Gen 1:26). Furthermore, he orders male and female to: "Be fruitful and multiply, and fill the earth and subdue it" (Gen 1:28).

The People of Genesis: A Blessed Human Nature

Both the attributes of dominion and the ability to subjugate portray humans as very powerful, political masters of the planet. Accepting this charge gives humans great responsibility, in addition to authority. On the face of it, humans, not God, make history. We will see later on that God fudges on this by powerfully intervening in human affairs—via those who hear his voice—to make history himself.

But the die is cast.

In the summer of 2013, my wife and I passed a church marquee in Camden, Maine, that read: "I've always wanted to ask God why He allows war, pestilence, poverty, and hatred to exist, but I'm afraid He would ask me the same question." The question of why God allows bad things to happen assumes that God can control everything. This assumption is really not part of the Judaic-Christian tradition. What is often called an act of God, such as an earthquake or hurricane, is not. There are natural laws that explain them, just as natural laws explain diseases. We social scientists have the task of explaining wars, racism, poverty, and crime. We do that on the assumption that their causes rest with human behavior and its flaws. Similarly, medical personnel act on the assumption that the causes of disease can be found in science.

In short, the Bible, including the oral tradition before it was written, is one of the first sources to give human beings great power and responsibilities.

But what else? And what is God's role in relation to human beings?

Answers lie in the allegory about the tree of the knowledge of good and evil, the fruit of which God tells Adam not to eat or he will die (Gen 2:17). But before Adam disobeys God by eating, God has him name every living creature, in effect, creating language and supplementing man's power to define his existence. At the risk of taking a ribbing, I will skip over the creation of woman. Eve, however, plays a big role in explaining to the Hebrews why humans are destined to die, why childbirth will be so painful, why many believe that husbands should rule over their wives (politics), and why we have to work to live (Gen 3:16–19).

Part I—The Hebrew Bible

Enter the snake, a talking snake, which is probably the representation of Eve's id—what psychoanalysts would say are her natural instincts and drives. The snake tells Eve that eating the forbidden fruit will not only not cause her death but also make her like God, knowing good and evil. Wanting to be wise like God—who wouldn't want to be?—Eve eats the tasty fruit and gives some to Adam. This gives rise to the consequences stated above—answers to questions that early humans not in the Garden of Eden clearly had to grapple with (Gen 3:1–7). This is also the story of the first group—a family—and man supposedly making decisions for the group. But here it is Eve, who is the first politician, persuading Adam to eat.

The story of Adam and Eve says much about human nature.

It explains free will. Before eating the forbidden fruit of the tree of the knowledge of good and evil, these two prototype humans have no capacity for choice, only animal instincts. However, when God warns them not to eat, he must have assumed that his creation would have and express free will, the ability to choose. After eating, they suddenly know that they are naked and cover themselves up (Gen 3:7). Then they have to react to conditions, themselves, and their environment. The necessity of choice requires free will. This human capability is especially necessary after their expulsion from the absolute abundance of the Garden of Eden. On the outside, there is a scarcity of food, security, knowledge, and social partners. Humans have to work for them. For example, their son Abel has to care for the sheep and their other son, Cain, has to till the ground (Gen 4:3). Scarcity also means that other humans will seek their needs and wants. The environment is competitive. As individuals, humans need some measure of self-concern and, as part of a group, concern for others. Here again, power is a necessary pursuit. The physical and human environment must comply with human aims to satisfy needs and wants.

The question of good and evil reappears. In a competitive environment (and this brief summary will not do the subject justice), giving or not giving everyone his or her due produces, respectively, good and evil, which is a key political concept for Greek political philosophers who expound on the subject of justice.

THE PEOPLE OF GENESIS: A BLESSED HUMAN NATURE

The predisposition that people believe humans have for doing good and evil shapes their attitudes toward human nature—good or bad and in what combination. To repeat, I will explain how these attitudes shape political ideologies and philosophies, which, in turn, shape political behavior.

This allegory in Genesis instructs humans about their condition. It is not history but, rather, a great tale explaining basic questions of life. However, God is not telling humans that they are on their own. God gets very chatty throughout the rest of the Hebrew Bible, even intervening whenever he feels it is necessary. Nevertheless, humans, by and large, are intended to control their own destiny. They ultimately have the power and the responsibility for it. That mix of Godly power and human behavior tells the story throughout the whole Bible and, for that matter, throughout history.

Not only do Adam and Eve eat of the forbidden fruit, leading to their expulsion from the Garden of Eden, Cain, one of their sons, slays Abel, his sibling. This says a lot about human nature as defined herein. Not surprisingly, here it is flawed. Humans are impulsive, selfish, disobedient, and violent.

The starting point of any political philosophy is its concept of human nature. If it is equally good and perverse, the task of government is to suppress bad behavior. Doing so, logically, lets good behavior flourish.

There are many ways for government to suppress bad behavior. One is favored in the Hebrew Bible. Laws are the dos and don'ts concerning behavior. They also prescribe a penalty if the laws are not obeyed and offer benefits if they are. Government earns its name if it can prescribe and interpret laws and enforce them. Government leaders can also educate the populace about proper cultural norms of behavior, thus mobilizing social pressure to ensure good behavior and discourage the bad. Besides laws, the leaders in the Hebrew Bible shape culture continually through the institution of sacrifices, ritual songs, ceremonies, oral history, and the strictures of prophets. Moses is the primal champion of both, as we will explicate in chapter 4. A related third technique that political leaders use to reduce bad behavior—defined as that which injures the innocent, harms the functioning of society and government, and puts the entire community at foreign risk—is also introduced in the Hebrew Bible. We moderns call it "checks and balances." It appears rather surprisingly in the Book of Exodus. There we find Moses and Aaron checking and balancing God, actually getting God to repent his wayward ways. Later on, prophets confront Israel's political leaders when they go astray.

At the conclusion of this chapter, I will illustrate some of the techniques that modern political philosophers have designed, based on those presented in the Hebrew Bible, to check bad behavior.

But what if human nature is essentially good? What, then, is the role of government to let it bloom in society?

There is more of a hint of good human nature in the story of Noah and later in that of Abraham.

Still, in Genesis, Noah, clearly a late bloomer at the age of 500 when his story begins, provides further instruction as to where power lies and what it is to be good-natured.

Noah is at that ripe age as father to Shem, Ham, and Japeth. They and other people multiply mightily. God observes them. He expresses little surprise but much hostility to humans when he sees their wickedness, evil, corruption, and violence. They ate of the tree, after all. God regrets that he made humans and decides to "blot out" his people (Gen 6:6–7). But wait—Noah finds favor in his eyes (Gen 6:8). He is righteous, blameless, and walks with God. God instructs Noah to construct a really big three-deck, spacious ark to house two of every living creature, and demanded that seven pairs of these animals be clean (Gen 7:1–4). How Noah is to get them is not explained, but he has to do so because all other living creatures will be killed in the worldwide flood.

Let me pause here. The land barrier between the Mediterranean and a smaller Black Sea broke sometime in ancient history, and archeologists have found the remains of human settlements on the floor of the now larger Black Sea. Oral stories of the flood were common when the Noah account was told and then written.

The People of Genesis: A Blessed Human Nature

The flood was local, not worldwide. So here is another allegory, a story of instruction.

After the flood recedes, as the story goes, Noah's sons' wives multiply and people the earth. Chapter 10 lists many of their offspring. Genealogy becomes very important for the Hebrews. They are to remember that they come from righteous stock. All the bad human stock drowned. Human nature, the story says, is basically good (or at least far more good than evil) because it comes from the righteous Noah. In addition, humans should strive to be good and work to punish evil.

Here is another needed function of government. If human nature is essentially good, then government's job is to remove the impediments that stifle goodness. The principal impediment in the Hebrew Bible is the lack of obedience to God. The prophets say this repeatedly. When the Israelites turn away from God and his laws, they become corrupted, and the Hebrew Bible states that goodness suffers and bad things—conquest and exile—happen.

The key point in the Hebrew Bible in tracing the humans from which they had sprung stipulates that the Hebrews have a terrific pedigree. Along with being God's chosen people, they are also inheritors of a virtuous human nature. This combination tells them that great things are not only possible but also expected and likely. They have a wonderful potential—from dominion and nature—that can be nurtured and realized. By implication, other peoples are not so blessed, although how they survived the flood is left unclear.

One does not have to be cynical to understand that creation stories, and those who create and interpret them, serve to enhance a people. Such is normal behavior. And if close to the reality, they are a belief that sets the stage for great politics and outcomes.

Whatever notion of human nature dominates in any political system will, therefore, shape the government's constitution.

The embodiment of the belief that human nature is largely perverse or just moderately so can be found in two strains of modern political thought.

Part I—The Hebrew Bible

For those who consider human nature severely on the bad side, there are the writings of Machiavelli (mainly *The Prince*, not his *Discourses*); orthodox Christian, Jewish, and Islamic ideologues; and political fascists. They emphasize draconian laws, severe punishments, and all-powerful rulers as the proper way to manage society. Bad behavior, which of course includes any challenges to the ruler's rule, must be crushed. The unwashed masses cannot be trusted. Untethered, they will be bad, very bad, and harmful to themselves and to society. Thus, for a political philosophy based on extremely flawed human nature, the people must be controlled severely.

The reader is probably thinking: Wait a minute! If human nature is so flawed, doesn't that make the nature of the autocratic rulers flawed as well? Precisely. Presumably, they are just as venal, self-centered, and misguided as they think their subjects are. Of course, these rulers think that they are different—superior persons, worthy of calling the shots. Policy advice, freedom of choice, democratic rights, and the market cannot be under the sway of the unwashed masses. Political fascists—whether Hitler, Mussolini, Franco, or Pinochet—all believed in their own superiority over the common people. Strangely, they also see their rule as necessary to usher in a glorious epoch for their people. The leaders have to severely direct and control the people in order to achieve their proper destiny. This makes ruling based on a perverse concept of human nature rather oppressive and bleak.

For more moderate political thinkers, who see both the good and bad in human nature, reliance on strict authority is not necessary. Yes, laws and constitutions are essential for proper rule, but so is liberty. As such, elections, the separation of powers, and checks and balances play essential roles. The writings of Thomas Hobbes, John Locke, Montesquieu, and the authors of the Federalist Papers hold sway. The people can be trusted on many things, including free speech and press, voting, and entrepreneurship.

The Federalist Papers—the writings of John Jay, Alexander Hamilton, and James Madison—were tailored for publication in newspapers in order to urge the various states to ratify the new

The People of Genesis: A Blessed Human Nature

U.S. Constitution that emerged from the Convention of 1787 in Philadelphia. Their main concern targets the decision of the New York state legislature, just as much a keystone state as Pennsylvania would claim. Failure in Albany would leave the United States divided in two.

Federalist No. 51 argued on the basis of a flawed but still worthy notion of human nature. Checking certain vices would bring good government.

Some key passages written by James Madison follow.

The Federalist Paper No. 51

The Structure of the Government Must Furnish the Proper Checks and Balances Between the Different Departments

TO WHAT expedient, then, shall we finally resort, for maintaining in practice the necessary partition of power among the several departments, as laid down in the Constitution? The only answer that can be given is, that as all these exterior provisions are found to be inadequate, the defect must be supplied, by so contriving the interior structure of the government as that its several constituent parts may, by their mutual relations, be the means of keeping each other in their proper places.

In order to lay a due foundation for that separate and distinct exercise of the different powers of government, which to a certain extent is admitted on all hands to be essential to the preservation of liberty, it is evident that each department should have a will of its own; and consequently should be so constituted that the members of each should have as little agency as possible in the appointment of the members of the others. Were this principle rigorously adhered to, it would require that all the appointments for the supreme executive, legislative, and judiciary magistracies should be drawn from the same fountain of authority, the people, through channels having no communication whatever with one another. Perhaps such a plan of constructing the several departments would be less difficult in practice than it may in contemplation appear. Some difficulties, however, and some additional expense would attend the execution of it. Some deviations, therefore, from the principle must be admitted. In the constitution of the judiciary department in particular, it might be inexpedient to insist rigorously on the principle: first, because peculiar qualifications being essential in the members, the primary consideration ought to be to select that mode of choice which best secures these qualifications; secondly, because the permanent tenure by which the appointments are held in that department, must soon destroy all sense of dependence on the authority conferring them.

It is equally evident, that the members of each department should be as little dependent as possible on those of the others, for the emoluments annexed to their offices. Were the executive magistrate, or the judges, not independent of the legislature in this particular, their independence in every other would be merely nominal. But the great security against a gradual concentration of the several powers in the same department, consists in giving to those who administer each department the necessary constitutional means and personal motives to resist encroachments of the others. The provision for defense must in this, as in all other cases, be made commensurate to the danger of attack. Ambition must be made to counteract ambition. The interest of the man must be connected with the constitutional rights of the place. It may be a reflection on human nature, that such devices should be necessary to control the abuses of government. But what is government itself, but the greatest of all reflections on human nature? If men were angels, no government would be necessary. If angels were to govern men, neither external nor internal controls on government would be necessary. In framing a government which is to be administered by men over men, the great difficulty lies in this: you must first enable the government to control the governed; and in the next place oblige it to control itself.

A dependence on the people is, no doubt, the primary control on the government; but experience has taught mankind the necessity of auxiliary precautions. This policy of supplying, by opposite and rival interests,

The People of Genesis: A Blessed Human Nature

> the defect of better motives, might be traced through the whole system of human affairs, private as well as public. We see it particularly displayed in all the subordinate distributions of power, where the constant aim is to divide and arrange the several offices in such a manner as that each may be a check on the other that the private interest of every individual may be a sentinel over the public rights. These inventions of prudence cannot be less requisite in the distribution of the supreme powers of the State. But it is not possible to give to each department an equal power of self-defense. In republican government, the legislative authority necessarily predominates. The remedy for this inconveniency is to divide the legislature into different branches; and to render them, by different modes of election and different principles of action, as little connected with each other as the nature of their common functions and their common dependence on the society will admit. It may even be necessary to guard against dangerous encroachments by still further precautions. As the weight of the legislative authority requires that it should be thus divided, the weakness of the executive may require, on the other hand, that it should be fortified.

Madison is concerned here with explaining the provisions for a separation of powers in the Constitution that are necessary for government to control the governed and itself. He and his fellow Federalists make the case that the various departments of government should be separate and dependent upon selection by the people. There is a qualification. The judiciary is not selected by the people, but its lifetime tenures serves to protect its independence. Being separate, the departments can check each other, because the process of making and enforcing law and policies generally requires all three functions—executive, legislative, and judicial. Madison states that "Ambition must be made to counteract ambition."

Note that Madison sees human nature as the basis for concepts of government, as do virtually all political theorists. He goes on to say, "But what is government itself, but the greatest reflections on human nature?"

He writes that a community of angels would need no government, thereby affirming that men, real men, have flaws. In addition, in the same view of human nature, he says, "If angels were to govern men, neither external nor internal controls on government would be necessary." As we will discover next, Karl Marx came close to this view when he declared that, under communism, the state would eventually "wither away."

In Federalist No. 10, the same author defends the federal government over the states by making the case that the larger the government, the less dominance the factions will have. Although a faction may gain political control in a single state, that faction will be checked by different factions and interests from other states.

There is no better explanation for checking perverse political behavior, be it by factions or a unified oppressive government, than The Federalist Papers. New York did, of course, ratify the Constitution.

But what of the opposite view of human nature?

This may surprise some readers, but Karl Marx exemplifies, in his political philosophy, the belief that human nature is overwhelmingly good. He focuses, above all, on removing the singular impediment to a good, humane society. That impediment is private property. He believes that it corrupts human goodness by imposing greed on the capitalist in terms of money and political power and by imposing wage slave labor on the proletariat. Communism, by promoting free labor "from each according to his ability and to each according to his needs," becomes, for him, "a specter haunting [the capitalist rulers of] Europe." A new age is coming. Because classes and the class struggle are based on those who control private property and those who are dependent upon those who control it, abolishing private property abolishes the class struggle. The exploitation of the workers—the proletariat—ends. With the end of the class struggle, all will be well, including the withering away of government.

The People of Genesis: A Blessed Human Nature

The key passages in Karl Marx and Frederick Engels' 1848 "Communist Manifesto" follow.

> The history of all hitherto existing society is the history of class struggles.
>
> The bourgeoisie, wherever it has got the upper hand, has put an end to all feudal, patriarchal, idyllic relations. It has pitilessly torn asunder the motley feudal ties that bound man to his "natural superiors", and has left remaining no other nexus between man and man than naked self-interest, than callous "cash payment". It has drowned the most heavenly ecstasies of religious fervour, of chivalrous enthusiasm, of philistine sentimentalism, in the icy water of egotistical calculation. It has resolved personal worth into exchange value, and in place of the numberless indefeasible chartered freedoms, has set up that single, unconscionable freedom—Free Trade. In one word, for exploitation, veiled by religious and political illusions, it has substituted naked, shameless, direct, brutal exploitation.
>
> But not only has the bourgeoisie forged the weapons that bring death to itself; it has also called into existence the men who are to wield those weapons—the modern working class—the proletarians.
>
> In proportion as the bourgeoisie, i.e., capital, is developed, in the same proportion is the proletariat, the modern working class, developed—a class of labourers, who live only so long as they find work, and who find work only so long as their labour increases capital. These labourers, who must sell themselves piecemeal, are a commodity, like every other article of commerce, and are consequently exposed to all the vicissitudes of competition, to all the fluctuations of the market.
>
> Of all the classes that stand face to face with the bourgeoisie today, the proletariat alone is a really revolutionary class. The other classes decay and finally disappear in the face of Modern Industry; the proletariat is its special and essential product.
>
> All the preceding classes that got the upper hand sought to fortify their already acquired status by subjecting society at large to their conditions of appropriation.

Part I—The Hebrew Bible

> The proletarians cannot become masters of the productive forces of society, except by abolishing their own previous mode of appropriation, and thereby also every other previous mode of appropriation. They have nothing of their own to secure and to fortify; their mission is to destroy all previous securities for, and insurances of, individual property.

Well, communism did eventually come to power in parts of Europe and elsewhere, resulting in brutal dictatorships when the goodness in humans—namely the rulers—turned out to be far from the ideal. The state did not "wither away," as Marx predicted. Far from it. It became what the Federalists had predicted—namely, that a singular, all-powerful government would, itself, deny liberty to the people and enrich its rulers.

In fairness, societies that rely too heavily on liberty and the free market also over-estimate the power of laissez-faire, open culture, and checks and balances to suppress bad behavior. The logic of totally free competition, whether in the economy or government, ends up with a monopoly. One competitor wins all. Modern democracies have had to add a good dose of regulation in order to promote social justice and good order. They have also promoted welfare on the mild socialist model. Human nature, again, is not all that benevolent. It should surprise no one that historical records indicate that near *economic* monopoly in society translates into near *political* monopoly, just as a near *political* monopoly translates into that monopoly's control of a near *economic* monopoly. Power begets power.

Finally, there is another lesson in Genesis—one that still resonates with those who see God as the master of the world. God creates and uses natural disasters to punish evildoers, as in Noah's flood—a convenient notion before scientific knowledge explaining the causes of floods, devastating winds, and earthquakes became known. Because all distinct people starting off need to have answers to the challenges confronting them, the Hebrew Bible was and still is the textbook providing them.

The People of Genesis: A Blessed Human Nature

And we should live as long as many biblical characters, such as Noah, who are reported to have not only lived a long time but also commanded nations and produced offspring. Virtue brings long life. Regardless, the Hebrew Bible is a repertoire of instructive stories, telling us about human nature and God—and, of course, politics.

The Hebrew view of human nature is closer to Marx's than to that of the Federalists. Their expectations soar. As we shall analyze in chapter 6, unrealistically high expectations by a people holding impossible dreams cause overreaction, grief, disappointment, and eventual disaster. This comes later in Jewish history. Taking into account the enormous challenges facing the Hebrews—escaping from Egypt, surviving in the wilderness, conquering the Promised Land, and creating and preserving a government and the people—believing in benefiting from God's power and their own goodness and capabilities serves them well. As noted at the beginning of this chapter, the Hebrews learn from the creation story that God has given them dominion over all living creatures in the land. Dominion implies dominance. Believing that one's people are a cut above others also has other consequences, as we will witness as the Israelites form, struggle, and fight their way to where God wants them to go. Those who believe that they are superior beings tend to treat lesser beings with contempt or worse. But perhaps this view of human nature is necessary for the Israelites if they are to overcome many of the obstacles put before them by other people.

Moses mobilizes the Israelites' belief in their superiority, very much in line with the inherent goodness of Noah and Abraham. In addition, God's chosen people have to be special and his aid in their struggles is proof of this fact.

First, the Hebrews are given title to the Promised Land.

—— CHAPTER 3 ——

God as Realtor: One Land, Two Peoples

POLITICS INEVITABLY CONCERNS LAND. A people and their government, even if nomads, need to have control of land. It provides for food and industry, homes for families, a place for a congenial society and culture, and for protection with fortifications. Government, therefore, has the prime task of securing and maintaining its territory.

The story of Abram—soon to be Abraham after God promises that he will father multitudes—has great implications to this day. It presages the birth of nations and God's title to land.

Abram arrives in the eleventh chapter of Genesis. God tells him to move and that he will make a great nation of his descendants. Furthermore, God gives them the land title to Canaan—a political gift that frames the entire Hebrew Bible.

The land issue becomes very prominent in biblical politics. The Torah—the Five Books of Moses—focuses heavily on a large family leaving one famished-ravaged land; entering and living in Egypt, which eventually becomes inhospitable; wandering in a land called wilderness; and, finally, conquering and inhabiting the Promised Land.

Abram goes to the land; he hears God promise him his patrimony.

God as Realtor: One Land, Two Peoples

After a military expedition that rescues his kinsman Lot and his women and household, Abram complains to God that he has no heirs—certainly a rational complaint after being promised that he would father a nation. God tells him that his descendants will number as the stars above.

The American TV soap opera *The Young and the Restless* cannot compare with what happens next. Abram's thus-far infertile wife, Sar'ai, tells Abram that it will be all right for him to sleep with Hagar, her Egyptian maid. This is a move that Sar'ai soon regrets; she treats the pregnant Hagar harshly and eventually her drives away. An angel of the Lord intercepts the fleeing Hagar, telling her to return to Abram and that she will, via her son, Ishmael, produce a multitude of descendants (Gen 16:1–12). And so begins the Arab tribe-to-nation that becomes the favorite of early Muslims.

The plot thickens. God promises that Abraham's wife will bear him a son, Isaac, who will also be the father of a great nation, God's people. A covenant is God's offer, in which every male descendant has to be circumcised (Gen 17:9–21). Sar'ai, God then commands, will henceforth be called Sara.

There are also connections here with modern politics. The first is circumcision—an ingenious way of establishing a group identity and loyalty among Hebrew males. All politics deals with a group; activity is clustered around its government. This ceremony establishes the identity of a valued group, resulting in a condition that every Hebrew male will daily recognize, making him part of a group that is different. One of many parallels in modern politics is the Pledge of Allegiance—a mandated ceremony in public schools. As we will note when analyzing politics in the Christian Bible, baptism and the Eucharist are analogous ceremonies maintaining identity.

The second connection with modern politics is this: God's covenant with Abraham is really a pact of mutual obligation by which a faithful people will receive God's protection. This closely parallels the social contract theory of government made by political philosophers. It, too, is a pact of mutual obligation, in which a

Part I—The Hebrew Bible

people are to be obedient to rulers and the rulers will then protect their people's rights.

Let us return to the crux of the two-people-one-land problem.

According to the story, God creates two great nations that are genealogically diverse but related. Both have the same patriarch, and both receive his blessing. One is given a covenant and, as we now know, is destined to hold different faiths and people to the same land. One nation still insists that God was and is their realtor; the other claims the land title from centuries of habitation there.

The reader might be wondering: What was God thinking?

Maybe having two peoples and one land was devised as a test. For centuries the two religious nations descended from Abram/Abraham co-existed in relative peace. Now they are flunking the test.

Or maybe religious authorities create facts that are congenial to their peoples—facts that give them an advantage in politics, war, economics, and social standing. If a people believe that God or gods are on their side, consider the effects. A challenge to what God decrees becomes a direct assault on their religion. People will fight to uphold what they say God demands. And fight they must, because what a religion's God decrees obviously favors one people, leaving others at a disadvantage. The disadvantaged resist, fighting back. Consequently, whenever God is seen as favoring one side or the other, conflict and violence are prescribed and inevitable. This pertains not only to Jews and Muslims; think about the Christian Crusades and the Muslim resistance that they spawned. Conflicting land titles, each given by God, is a recipe for conflict.[6]

From the time of Abraham onward, the Hebrew Bible is filled with war. Much of this is related to controlling land.

Chapters 4 through 6 will analyze its politics. They will reveal a spectacular beginning of Israelite politics and the establishment of their state in the Promised Land; they conclude with their political denouement. The Jewish state is no more. God's hidden politics appears with Jesus. His political agenda is masked by his creation of a new religion, but that religion has a definite political agenda.

God as Realtor: One Land, Two Peoples

The case will be made, when the Christian Bible is analyzed, that the subversion of Rome is the Christian political aim. For the Jews, the political issue of their land has had a long life, stretching to this day.

There is no question that the Jewish diaspora—the expulsion of Jews from Roman Palestine—put Jews in foreign societies that were at times congenial and at times harsh. Anti-Semitism, arising from jealousy of the enterprise and, as we will argue later, the cultural superiority of local Jews, their clannishness, and the (bogus) charge that they killed Christ, made life precarious for Jews. Forced conversions to Christianity or expulsion resulted in a massive Jewish migration from fifteenth century Spain. Pogroms in nineteenth and twentieth century Russia, Poland, and elsewhere in Europe led to a large Jewish migration to the United States. And the 1895 Dreyfus Affair in France produced the movement to reconstitute Israel in the Promised Land. Theodore Herzl, the movement's author, saw the unjust prosecution of Captain Alfred Dreyfus (a Jew) as a German spy to be proof that Jews could never be at home unless they were living in their original homeland. In 1895, he began publicizing the necessity of a Jewish state. Hitler's Holocaust sealed the issue for many European Jews. They flooded British-controlled Palestine before, during, and after World War II.

There may have been a people without a land then, but there certainly was not a land without a people, contrary to what Christian "Restorationists" proclaimed in the nineteenth and twentieth centuries as justifying the Jews' reclaiming Palestine. Although it is one of the most oft-cited phrases in the literature of Zionism, there is little evidence that Jewish Zionists used the phrase "A land without a people for a people without a land." Nevertheless, it is still widely attributed to Jews who advocated a Jewish state (and were usually opponents to Zionism), in order to denigrate Jewish return to British-controlled Palestine.

Clashes with the resident Muslim and Christian Arabs erupted as soon as the Jewish population expanded its land holdings and influence. Everything came to a head after the massive

Part I—The Hebrew Bible

immigration of Jews after World War II. Jewish militants used terror against the occupying colonial British to force their withdrawal, which they did in 1948. The United Nations then divided Palestine into Jewish and Arab areas. This did not suit Palestine's neighbors—especially Egypt and Jordan—whose forces then attacked Jewish positions. Alas, with great skill, determination, and Soviet Bloc arms from Czechoslovakia, the Jewish forces repelled the attack. A UN-brokered ceasefire ended round one of hostilities in 1949. Jordan controlled and later annexed the West Bank of the Jordan River, including the Old City of Jerusalem, and Egypt controlled the Gaza Strip. Palestinians, both Muslim and Christian, who were as Abrahamic as the Jews, were now divided and under the political authority of foreign governments.

The Soviet Union and the United States quickly recognized the new state of Israel in 1948. The Soviets were motivated by anti-British imperialism; the Truman administration was motivated by an admiration of the Jewish achievement after the Holocaust and by the need for Jewish votes in the 1948 presidential election.

A list of all the military operations by Israel since the war for independence follows. The reader is invited to further investigate the circumstances for each, as that is beyond our scope here. However, each instance is related to either preserving Israeli land from attack (or presumed attack) or to expanding Israeli land. The political use of the military is frequent.

- 1956: The Suez War, in which Israel in cooperation with Britain and France (to regain control of the Suez Canal nationalized by Egypt) sought to control the Sinai Peninsula. President Eisenhower forced all three attacking parties to give up whatever gains they made in order to prevent a Soviet Cold War entrée to a receptive Arab world.
- 1967: The Six-Day War, in which Israel, fearing an apparent but actually phantom joint Arab attack, brilliantly defeated Egypt and occupied Gaza and the Sinai, defeated Jordan and occupied the West Bank, and defeated Syria and occupied the Golan Heights, one attack right after the other.

God as Realtor: One Land, Two Peoples

- 1967–70: The War of Attrition, in which mainly Egyptian incursions into the lands that Israel occupied brought about armed conflicts.

- 1973: The Yom Kippur War, also called the Ramadan War, in which Egypt struck, in a surprise attack across the Suez Canal, in an effort to break the status quo and provoke diplomacy in order to regain the Sinai. Peace efforts at Camp David by Egyptian President Anwar Sadat and President Carter, and Israeli Prime Minister Menachem Begin (who wanted to divide the Arab world via a peace treaty with Egypt) bore fruit in 1979. Israel withdrew from the Sinai, Israel and Egypt received guaranteed billions annually in U.S. grants, and Israel and Egypt exchanged ambassadors.

- 1982: The Lebanon War, in which Prime Minister Begin, in conjunction with Lebanon's Christian president, forged a plan to drive out the Palestinians and the Syrian forces in Lebanon. Israel's greater goal focused on creating a wider war—one in which Syria would occupy Jordan and make it a Palestinian country (its descendants already a majority there) in order to attack Israel, thereby allowing Israel to transfer, or expel, the Palestinians from the West Bank to their new homeland in Jordan. The plan broke down when the Lebanese Christians reneged on their part of the operation. Much of this plan, called Peace for Galilee II, is still a highly kept secret. Israel occupied southern Lebanon.

- 1981: An Israeli air strike on Iraq's nuclear reactor.

- 1982–2000: Engagement by Israeli forces in intermittent combat with Lebanese militias—Sunni, Shia, and Druze fighters, but mainly the Shia's Hezbollah and Amal.

- 1987–93: The First Intifada, in which Palestinian fighters used terrorism to protest their occupation.

- 2000–2005: The Second Intifada and the 2005 withdrawal from Gaza.

Part I—The Hebrew Bible

- 2006: The Lebanon War, in which Israel attacked to crush the militias and protect its northern border. With inconclusive results but high costs for both sides, it faded into a stalemate. Israel withdrew from Lebanon in 2009.
- 2008–2009: The Gaza War, in which rockets from Hamas-controlled Gaza rained on Israel, and Israeli air strikes reached the point where Israeli forces moved into Gaza proper.
- 2012: Operation Pillar of Defense against Gaza.
- 2014: Another Gaza war against Hamas.

That Israel has been militarily active is an understatement. Much of the activity has been provoked by hostile neighbors and the disgruntled occupied Palestinians who seek their own state, their own land. Other operations began as opportunities to expand. Israel, for example, now controls roughly 60 percent of the West Bank, leaving the rest under tenuous Palestinian Authority control.

An additional factor looms in its militarization—one that is reinforced by history.

The Holocaust tells Israelis that "never again" will Jews be put in a genocidal situation. They will be armed and dangerous. Israel, the only nuclear-armed state in the Middle East, reportedly has some 200–400 weapons. What is rarely analyzed is the early highly military history of the Hebrew people during their forty years in the wilderness, their conquest of Canaan, and the wars that followed. They were an archetypal warrior nation and an initially successful one. Israelis remember their original birth in war and seek to re-establish that success.

And that is where we turn in chapter 5.

The military exploits of the Israelites under the stunningly brilliant leadership of Joshua make an exceptional story of militarized politics.

The story of Abraham illustrates the intense political connection of a people to a particular land. Author Bruce Feiler calls

God as Realtor: One Land, Two Peoples

God's "sacred covenant of territory" through Abraham, Isaac, and Jacob one in which "the relationship between the people of Israel and the Promised Land is forged."[1] This solemn, binding agreement is never abrogated anywhere in the Bible. Land is also so important to life that it spurs powerful interests and the intention to gain, regain, and maintain control of it. This fact underlies the entire history of the Hebrew people and is one to which they are still intensely wedded. As we will analyze when the Christian Bible is the subject, Christianity breaks that devotion to just the Promised Land and could not exist if it had not. Its sights focus on a much wider playing field.

In addition to the ever-present land issue, the role of Abraham as the patriarch of two, eventually three, religions establishes the starting point of the eventual global dominance (at least in the West and South) of monotheism. That the three religions worshipping the same God are destined to clash cannot be attributed to God. The Bible contains no—I repeat, no—evidence of God telling Jews or Christians to fight each other. Even the Qur'an—the message of God via the angel Gabriel to Muhammad—calls for Muslims to treat Jews and Christians benignly, as "people of the book."

The conflicts among the three religions throughout history, therefore, have to be attributed to bad politics, where political leaders crassly use religion to "justify" their political ambition to stay in power and conquer others. All this, of course, includes the notion that they are defending the faith, with the leaders loudly proclaiming that God is on their side.

Here again we can see the intimate connection between religion and politics. Any belief system—whether fascism, communism, tribalism, traditionalism, or even democracy—can be used as a tool to unite and direct a people to engage in conflict. Religion just happens to be one of the ideological weapons (if not the original) for bad politics.

God, however, is heard clearly calling for war against those who have other gods. Canaan and its inhabitants are the target. Joshua is his instrument.

1. Feiler, *Walking the Bible: A Journey Through the Five Books of Moses*, 39.

CHAPTER 4

Moses: A Template for Political Leadership

MOSES HAS TO BE considered one of the most famous and effective political leaders in history. He is, after all, essentially a politician. He gets Israelite politics off to a brilliant start.

Moses' principal task consists of forming and leading a powerful nation—taking the Israelites out of Egypt and preparing them to conquer the Promised Land. Transmitting and enforcing God's religion—heavily legalistic—constitutes his second, equally important task. Although not originating with him, his religious job is still highly political. He is a law giver.

The book of Exodus begins, as is customary in the Hebrew Bible, with the genealogy of Israel—the people who came down to Egypt with Jacob (Israel) during the famine. I will abbreviate the story of Isaac's sons, Esau and Jacob, which is told in Genesis. Their rivalry, their many offspring, and Jacob's ascendancy after wrestling with an angel are keys to the creation of the principal political group in the Hebrew Bible. Jacob wins the wrestling match. God renames him Israel, signifying his destiny to create God's children (Exod 32:28–29). His wives have twelve sons, including Joseph, who is sold to the Ishmaelites by his brothers and ends up with some stature in Egypt. There, Jacob (Israel) and his family, fleeing

Moses: A Template for Political Leadership

famine in Canaan and being reunited with Joseph, live for decades. Their descendants resided there much longer.

Exodus notes that the "descendants of Israel were fruitful . . . so that the land was filled with them" (Exod 1:1–7).

This worries Pharaoh, who wonders if the people of Israel, so numerous, might side with Egypt's enemies in war. So he oppresses them with slave labor and orders the Hebrew midwives to kill newborn males. They fail to do so, and the Hebrews multiply some more. Pharaoh then orders that all newborn Hebrew males be cast into the Nile.

Enter a baby, his basket in the bulrushes, and his rescue by Pharaoh's daughter. She names him Moses.

When he grows up, a favorite of the royal family, Moses somehow knows that he is part of the Hebrew nation. It is not explained. One day, the story continues, he goes out and sees an Egyptian beating a Hebrew and Moses kills the Egyptian. Fearing that Pharaoh will find out, Moses flees to Midian. There he marries, has sons, and is visited by God. Moses is charged by God to take his oppressed people of Israel out of Egypt into Canaan, a land of milk and honey (Exod 3:4–12).

A comment is needed here. The reasons that God chooses Moses to lead the Hebrews out of Egypt, although somewhat obvious, are not mentioned. Moses knows the language and protocol of Pharaoh's court; is known to the royal family; and, unlike any other Hebrew, is best able to get an audience with Pharaoh. Moses is not the only perfect choice, he is God's *only* choice. The fact that Moses has a smart, articulate older brother, Aaron, is a bonus.

So begins the story of Moses and his spectacular leadership. The first part of this chapter will deal with his establishment as the leader of the oppressed Hebrews. Later, I will recount and analyze his brilliant political leadership in the long wanderings to Canaan.

Moses (in Midian) asks God what he should do to get the Israelites to accept him as their leader (Exod 3:11–22). "If I say that the God of your fathers has sent me," Moses wants to know, they will ask, "What is his name?" God says to tell them, "I AM has sent me to you." This, in Hebrew tradition, indicates a genuine statement from God.

Moses, following God's command, is to take the elders of Israel to Pharaoh, tell him of God's empowerment, and request that he allow the Hebrews to go on a three-day journey into the wilderness. Pharaoh will refuse, of course. Moses will then promise to smite the Egyptians and do wonders. Still Moses has doubts. That is when God makes his staff become a serpent when cast on the ground. Another sign will be a leprous hand that Moses can inflict upon himself and then cure by putting it into his bosom. Magic will do the trick. In addition, God will help Moses with his speech as well as with that of his more fluent brother, Aaron. If the miracles don't work, God says to tell Pharaoh that he will slay Egypt's first-born sons (Exod 3:13–22, 4:1–24).

Moses and Aaron gather the elders. Aaron recounts what God has charged. Moses does his miracles, and the people believe—as well they had to. He convinces them that he is from God (Exod 4:27–31).

Leaders need a source of legitimacy. Getting it is their first task. God is a familiar source in autocratic systems. Representing popular political ideologies is another. Whether among the Hebrews, Roman emperors, medieval European kings, Chinese dynasties, or even in Iran's Islamic Republic today, a belief that a leader is God's chosen one is a powerful source of legitimacy. Combined with primogeniture, it is even more powerful. In democratic systems, elections work to provide legitimacy.

Leaders in God's name can then say to the people, as Moses does, that God will lead them out of Egypt. If everyone believes, who could then doubt that it will occur?

Moses and Aaron go before Pharaoh and tell him God's message: "Let my people go." Well, Pharaoh increases his repression after denying Moses' and Aaron's request, which breaks the spirit of the Hebrews (Exod 6:6–9)

The rod-to-snake trick fails to move Pharaoh, as does turning the Nile red, killing the fish, and making the river water non-potable (Exod 7:10–24). A plague of frogs produces a decision by

Moses: A Template for Political Leadership

Pharaoh to let the people go if the plague is removed. The plague is removed but the Egyptian ruler reneges (Exod 8:13–15). And then he does so again and again—after an infestation of gnats and flies, a killer disease of his livestock, a dust that induces boils, a hailstorm, a plague of locusts that eats all the vegetation, and a three-day solar eclipse. Finally, the next plague does the trick. Until then, Pharaoh is indeed hard-hearted. The death of all the firstborn sons in Egypt, although the wrath of God passes over the Hebrews, finally softens the ruler's heart and the Egyptian people give the Hebrews silver, gold, and clothing to send them on their way (Exod 8:16—12:50).

The Passover is celebrated by Jews to this day. It is a festival remembering liberation.

Moses thus solidifies his rule over the Hebrews. He does so by defining a goal that is of prime importance to all the people and then singularly employs a strategy in a league with the Almighty to attain it. Moses has always said to all that he is doing God's will, speaking for God. In short, he delivers. Note also that he, with Aaron as his number two, consults and informs the elders of the twelve Israelite tribes (founded on Jacob's twelve sons) so that they support him in all his efforts, as do the Hebrew people.

The vastly underrated President Dwight Eisenhower defined leadership as the ability to get others to want what you want; Moses practices it millennia before. For the elders and the people, suffering for a great cause can be borne. A properly rated leader, Winston Churchill, knew this and, promising blood, sweat, toil, and tears in World War II as the price that had to be paid, mobilized the British people to not only endure but win the war.

This story also illustrates the belief that God is the maker of history and humans are his obedient team. That belief and the original one of man's dominion persist, with man's (and now woman's) dominion gaining dominance due to scientific progress. No wonder that some consider faith and science to be at odds. But perhaps, as the story of the Exodus relates, God works through humans, inspires them, gives them power and perseverance, and lets them do more of the work as they become more capable on their own. They were not very capable at the time of Moses.

Well, it's a thought.

The people go. As the people of Israel depart, Moses, obeying what God tells him to do, commands that the people eat only unleavened bread for seven days. Smart. Moses suspects, correctly, that Pharaoh will again renege and come after them. Time is of the essence. As Exod 12:39 relates, the people "could not tarry" to allow bread to leaven.

Good timing is also the mark of an exceptional leader. I am reminded of what my stepfather's friend, diplomat George Kennan, noted about the timing of his famous 1947 journal article, which largely defined the U.S. Cold War strategy of containment. He wrote that if it had been published six months earlier it would have been dismissed as premature and six months later as old hat.[1] Here, Moses' timing has to keep the people moving at a fast pace.

Indeed, as told in Exodus, Pharaoh and his aides soon miss the services of the "six-hundred thousand men on foot, besides women and children" who are fleeing Egypt (Exod 12:37).

Wise leaders also cultivate and nurture ceremony. It builds community, teaches history, and sets a people apart. Moses, following God's command, quickly establishes two ceremonies—the consecration of the first-born and seven days of eating only unleavened bread (Exod 13:1–10).

As far as the path to Canaan, Moses chooses not to go through the land of the Philistines, which is nearby, for a good reason. His people are unprepared for war with the fierce and numerous Philistines, and so, to avoid a fight, would want to return to the relative security of Egypt. Instead, Moses leads them to the Red Sea.

Pharaoh pursues with 600 charioteers and other horsemen. A strong wind pushes out the water, and the Israelites walk across, followed by the Egyptian forces. Although the muddy seafloor must have been suitable for walkers and flocks, it is not for heavy chariots and mounted horses. The wheels and horses become mired in the mud and the pursuing Egyptians are stopped cold.

---

1. X (Kennan), "The Sources of Soviet Conduct," 566–82.

Moses: A Template for Political Leadership

They become trapped when the wind stops and the waters return. This episode further cements the people's belief in Moses' leadership and the power of the Lord (Exod 14:1–31).

The Israelites create a song to describe and commemorate the triumph, which, like a ceremony, brings a spirit of pride and unity.

Life is undoubtedly hard and severe in the desert wilderness, and Moses, with God's help, provides more water and food when both run out. He also establishes the Sabbath day so that the people can rest.

Still, the people of Israel are not used to hardship and are not confident and strong. They complain a lot. Moses creates a test for them—one designed to toughen them up and give them confidence. With Moses cheering them on, the Israelites, under their military commander Joshua, defeat the Amalek, a clan blocking their path and apparently not a very fierce one. As with big-time college sports teams, which routinely schedule weak teams to play at the beginning of their schedules in order to nurture teamwork and create a habit and record of winning, Moses practices the same thing. So far, Moses' leadership has been flawless, but it also has been burdensome. His father-in-law, Jethro, offers a solution. Near Midian, his family, including his wife and sons, joins the Israelites. After observing all of the cases that Moses has to deal with and judge, Jethro suggests that he appoint trusted subordinates to manage the routine cases. Moses agrees, keeping only the hard cases (Exod 18:13–27). These subordinates lead groups of thousands, hundreds, fifties, and tens.

Wise leaders are open to and take good advice.

The people of Israel are taking shape. Their structure of a government—an essential political move—is in place. People have complained for millennia about the workings of government bureaucracies, but government cannot function without workers advising leaders, administering policies, and enforcing laws.

Next comes the hard part for any political leader and people—making laws and policies.

Moses becomes the law giver. The reader—myself included—must, at this point, deal with the presentation of God as talking

Part I—The Hebrew Bible

to Moses, as he did with Adam, Eve, Noah, and Abraham. God is portrayed as the master thinker and decider, with a commanding voice. And these human beings tell everyone that what they say comes from God.

So, who, at this point in our analysis, is really going to be the law giver?

Consider these thoughts: We must remember that many centuries of oral tradition pass down these stories. People at that time are really good about repeating stories generation after generation. Think of the Greeks and the stories of Homer, with many generations speaking them before they were ever written down. It should not surprise us that the people of Israel, in their oral tradition, would report God's words as just that; after all, Moses says that he is saying what God has told him to say and do. In addition, the Israelites are God's people. Of course he speaks to them and leads them.

Is this strange? Why, you may wonder, is God so silent in what Christians call the New Testament? Well, He has Jesus. But Jesus and those around him, according to my amateur mind, only hear God's words twice—at his christening and at the temptations at the mount. Jesus does, however, commune with the Father. More to the point, if Jesus says that he is doing what God tells him to do, then Jesus is not divine, not God incarnate. He would have only the status of a Moses. That, for Christians, would chop off one-third of the Trinity. I will have a lot more to say about God's role, however commanding, when the New Testament politics are analyzed.

And we, too, have that small voice that, seemingly independent of us, speaks to us. Freud has a word for it: the super ego. It tells us to marry that guy, don't fly on that airplane today, you've got to pay the rent, and the like. So, let's treat the stories as we have—as the characters in the Hebrew Bible hearing God and speaking in his name. The key evidence of hearing God is proof that he speaks.

The reader may wonder if the characters in biblical stories sometimes make up what God tells them in order to gain credibility, compliance, and stature. I do sometimes. It's natural to be skeptical, and I will note when this is likely.

Back to our story.

Moses: A Template for Political Leadership

Moses, on the advice of his father-in-law, has organized the people of Israel under his subordinate judges (more on political leaders as judges later on in the analysis). We must also remember that the people have no political tradition or experience in independent self-government, that they are intensely clannish and quarrelsome, and that they have little idea about what to do or not do. As a modern American cliché would note, they don't have a clue. Hence, the need for God to tell them what to do or not do and, most pressing, the need for laws.

Called by Moses to the foot of Mount Sinai, the people gather after the third new moon of their wandering. God tells Moses that they shall not ascend with Moses and Aaron lest they die (Exod 19:6–25). God speaks the Ten Commandments to Moses.

What is interesting is the fact that the first four commandments enshrine God as the leader, saying that he is above all other gods, demanding that no graven image be bowed down to, and stating that his name shall not be taken in vain (Exod 20:1–7). God has to be first in Israelite life. Laws regulating behavior follow, all reflecting the proper way to keep the people of Israel communal, secure, and internally just.

Their politics are maturing.

Judaism is a religion heavily weighted with law. This reflects the fact that the people of Israel are starting from scratch as an independent people needing guidance. Law provides it and tradition keeps it.

In contrast, as we shall explore further later on, Christianity forms in established cultures (plural), which already have laws and customs. There was less need for a comprehensive set of guidelines. In many ways, Islam is more like Judaism than Christianity, for the people that Muhammad creates and leads are a new people who need to receive a new set of instructions. Those instructions, which the angel Gabriel gives to Muhammad, are in the Qur'an.

God, after giving his commandments, provides Moses with a very long set of ordinances about slavery and crime. Many of the remedies for crimes require the death penalty, including such crimes as murder and even striking or cursing one's parents. Such

Part I—The Hebrew Bible

severe measures must be thought necessary to keep the unruly, uncivilized (not abiding in a city milieu), and impressionable people in line. The ordinances go on to include hospitality, finance, sacrifices, and good customs (Exod 21, 22, 23:1–19).

God promises to give the commandments on tablets of stone and tells Moses to again climb the mountain, where he stays for forty days and forty nights (Exod 12:24). Once there, Moses is ordered to prepare a tabernacle with an ark, a table, and other things for it, and priests to service it (Exod 24:12–18, 25—28:1).

Forty days and forty nights is a long time for a leader to be absent. The Israelites—a weak and insecure people—need a leader. They go to Aaron and ask him to make gods to go before them.

So begins one of the most instructive stories in the Hebrew Bible—one that I often used in my political science classes at the colleges where I taught. It is the golden calf lesson.

Actually, the story has many lessons.

The first is the lesson to stop the people of Israel from alienating themselves. Aaron tells the people to take off their golden earrings and give them to him. He then fashions a molten calf, saying that these are the gods that brought them out of Egypt. Aaron decrees that the next day will be a feast. The people bring burnt offerings to the calf, after which they sit down to eat, drink, and play (Exod 32:1–6).

God, on the mountain with Moses, knows what is happening below and, of course, burns hot. He tells Moses that the people "have corrupted themselves" (Exod 32:7–8). They are "stiffnecked," which I interpret to mean that they are incapable of correct behavior.

Here is my (and no doubt others') interpretation of this event.

God wants the people of Israel to be strong. Instead, they have taken part of themselves—their earrings—and made a god. In effect, they have transferred their strength to an external thing, giving the calf their power. They have also created a false god—actually, no god at all. This is a clear case of alienation or estrangement. God also wants them to be faithful to the real God.

Moses: A Template for Political Leadership

Back on the mountain, God tells Moses that, as for your people, "I may consume them."

What follows is the first instance in which a human argues with God, pleading for his people and trying to change God's mind. His argument notes that if they are consumed the Egyptians will ask: "Why did he lead them forth only to slay them in the mountains?" Moses actually tells God "to repent of this evil against thy people." He asks God to remember Abraham, Isaac, and Israel and the promises made to them to multiply and give to them the Promised Land.

God repents (Exod 32:11–14).

As I read it, God is allowing his people to be more authoritative, more in control, and become a more mature community while still remaining God's people.

Back to alienation.

When Moses comes down the mountain and sees the dancing and the calf, his "anger burns hot." After throwing down the tables, he takes the calf, grinds it to powder, adds water, and makes the people drink it (Exod 32:19–20). Moses thereby makes the Israelites whole again, restoring the power to them that they gave away, alienated, to the calf.

Moses doesn't stop there. He asks whoever is on the Lord's side to come to him. The sons of Levi come; put on swords as Moses commands; and slay every wayward man, his brother, companion, and neighbor—3,000 in all. God also sends a plague of an uncertain nature upon the people (Exod 32:25–35).

God then tells Moses to depart to the Promised Land of milk and honey, but without God's leadership, lest he consume his stiff-necked people. An angel will do the job.

More power and responsibility are therefore given to the people.

There are more of God's decrees.

The book of Leviticus—the Levis are keepers of the tabernacle—is loaded with God giving Moses, at Mount Sinai, a variety of religious decrees and good advice to pass along to the Israelites.

God concludes with a promise if his words are followed and a warning if they are not.

Leviticus starts off with a long list of decrees about how to conduct burnt offerings and sacrifices, taking all of the first ten chapters. This initially puzzled me. Why? After some thought, it seems to me that decreeing these offerings is designed to cement the close relationship between God and the people of Israel.

To sacrifice animals and grains to God compels those doing the offering to value highly the object of the offering. Here, in effect, the people of Israel are making an investment in God. He has to be of great value. He has to be supported, worshipped, and pleased, if one is to believe that God controls the destiny of his people. The various sacrifices are ritualized for one very good reason: They need to endure, and the best way to have behavior endure is to create a set way to do it over and over. Hence, for political effect, make it a ritual.

For example, here is what God tells Moses about just one of the offerings:

> If a man's offering is a sacrifice of peace offering, if he offers an animal from the herd, male or female, he shall offer it without blemish before the Lord. And he shall lay his hand upon the head of his offering and kill it at the door of the tent of meeting; and Aaron's sons the priests shall throw the blood against the altar round about. And from the sacrifice of the peace offering, as an offer by fire to the lord, he shall offer the fat covering the entrails and all the fat that is on the entrails, and the two kidneys with the fat that is on them at the loins, and the appendage of the liver which he shall take away with the kidneys. Then Aaron's sons shall burn it on the altar upon the burnt offering, which is upon the wood on the fire; it is an offering by fire, a pleasing odor to the Lord. (Lev 3:1–5)

Note that there is a definite cost to the offering. The man making the offering sacrifices one of his herd—not an insignificant loss. Psychologists say that the greater the cost for something, the more that something is valued. The ritual is rather precise, and that it's pleasing to God is also stated.

Moses: A Template for Political Leadership

God gives some practical advice in Leviticus as well, two pieces of which seem noteworthy.

Dietary laws are found in chapter 11. "Whatever parts the hoof and is cloven-footed and chews the cud, among the animals, you may eat. Nevertheless, among those that chew the cud or part the hoof, you shall not eat these" (Lev 11:3-4). The camel, rock badger, hare, and the swine are thus said to be unclean. All these, of course, are edible, but it is their function that makes their uncleanness good advice. Take the camel. Does it make any sense to eat one's efficient transportation vehicle? The camel is perfect for desert travel, and the people of Israel are destined to travel there. Or the swine, an animal whose diet is close to that of humans? Does it make any sense to raise a competitive eating animal when food in the desert is so scarce?

A parallel prescription is found in the Hindu faith, where the eating of beef is proscribed. In India, does it make any sense to eat your farm tractor, milk producer, and fuel for the cooking fire (dried dung)?

I am somewhat at a loss as to why food in the waters must have "fins and scales" (Lev 11:12). Perhaps every other animal is a bottom feeder, whose diet is an abomination.

There is even some very good horticulture advice in Leviticus. God says, "When you reap the harvest of the land, you shall not reap your field to its very border, neither shall you gather the gatherings of your harvest" (Lev 19:9). The first rule is designed to prevent valuable, scarce top soil from washing away in a rainstorm, and the second refurbishes the soil. Both practices are widespread today.

The people of Israel really need structure and a good set of laws and policies. Creating a constitution can provide it. In contrast, African-Americans freed from slavery suffered a structure that was not progressive or beneficent. The point is that essentially needed structure, with its shape and wisdom, molds a people's political destiny—maybe not forever, but for a long time.

Near the end of Leviticus, God lets Moses and the people of Israel know what will happen if his decrees are violated.

Part I—The Hebrew Bible

It reminds me of a personal experience. As the newly elected mayor of a small city in Iowa decades ago, I introduced and proposed a new ordinance (I can't remember the subject) to City Council. I knew that it would pass, because it would bring clear benefits to the citizens at very low cost. The city attorney quickly interjected, asking, "What happens if people violate it?" The penalty for violating the ordinance had not been included. Government law needs a punishment attached to tell people what will happen if it is violated. Such a penalty—clearly something to be avoided—encourages compliance.

God did not make my mistake.

Chapter 26 states the benefits that God will bring "If you walk in my statutes and observe my commandments and do them." The list (Lev 26:1–13) includes the following:

- Rains and fertile land and abundant crops
- A secure land of peace
- An absence of evil beasts
- The defeat of your enemies
- You will be fruitful and multiply
- God will walk among you, who has made you walk erect

These are very attractive benefits, no doubt. But laws and statutes do get broken, incurring some very severe costs that God will inflict.

Here is what God promises to do to the people of Israel "if you do not hearken to me, and will not do these commandments, if you spurn my statutes, and if your soul abhors my ordinances" (Lev 26:14–46):

- Terror, consumption, fever, and loss of life
- Your enemies will eat your crops, defeat you, and rule over you
- Crop failures and famine
- Plagues and wild beast that will eat your children and cattle

Moses: A Template for Political Leadership

- Be forced to cannibalism
- Cities destroyed
- Exile and forced labor

The last punishment has an addendum of hope. Upon confession, becoming humble, and making amends, God will restore the covenant, remember the land, and be their God. And, of course, this happens.

Counting and timing are political necessities.

The book of Numbers opens in the second year of the wanderings, when God tells Moses to take a census of the people, by tribe, except for the Levites, who, under Aaron, manage the tabernacle. When the total of the twelve tribes is tallied, 603,550 Israelite males twenty years of age and older are counted. No need to guess why the book is titled "Numbers." Again, note that numbers given in the Hebrew Bible exhibit general size or multitude, not exactness.

Like the genealogy noted earlier, the census reminds the people of Israel that they are a people, distinct and numbered. Their roots are to be remembered; their bloodlines upheld; and their unity preserved. This makes political governance easier for their leaders.

Following the census and some sacrifices, God gives Moses a blessing to the people of Israel—one famous to this day and used often in Christian services as well, which reads: "The Lord bless you and keep you; the Lord make his face to shine upon you, and be gracious to you; the Lord lift up his countenance upon you, and give you peace" (Num 6:24–26). And so God's name is again put upon the people—an everlasting reminder.

Later in the book of Numbers, there is an important turning point in the wanderings to the Promised Land. Very near Canaan, the Lord tells Moses to send out some men—one leader from every tribe—to spy out the land of Canaan. They are charged by Moses to find if the people there are strong or weak, few or many, whether the land is good or bad, cities are camps or strongholds, the land is rich or poor, and whether there is wood in it. The spies return after forty days and report, first showing Moses, Aaron, and all the people the grapes, pomegranates, and figs they have brought back with them. Proof, they say, that the land flows with milk and honey. So far, so well and good. "Yet the people who dwell in the land are strong," the spies report, "and the cities are fortified and very large." They identify the descendants of Anak—tribes inhabiting the Negeb, hill country, and by the sea and along the Jordan (Num 13:1–29).

Caleb, one of the spies, then takes the floor. "Let us go up at once, and occupy it; for we are well able to overcome it." Most of rest of the spies do not agree, citing that "they are stronger than we" and so many. Hearing this, the people raise a loud cry and weep, murmuring against Moses and Aaron. They question the leaders, asking why they were brought out of Egypt only to be defeated. Let us go back to Egypt, they cry. The spies Joshua and Caleb try to rally the people, pleading with them not to rebel against the Lord or fear the people of the land, for God will be with us. All to no avail (Num 13:30–33; 14:1–10).

God appears to Moses. He tells Moses that the people must despise and not believe in him. He threatens to "strike them with pestilence and disinherit them." Moses again talks God out of it. God then says that those who did not harken to his voice will not make it to the Promised Land; Caleb, Joshua, their descendants, and those under twenty years of age will. For every day of spying (forty) God says that the people of Israel will spend forty years wandering before entering Canaan. But some of the people go into the hill country, against the advice of Moses, and are defeated (Num 14:11–45). Moses and Aaron are still not out of the woods, so to speak, for a large group of people led by tribal leader Korah charges them with arrogance. God soon makes quick work of them, burying Korah and his men alive and consuming the others in a fire. Still other rebels are killed by a plague before God stops it upon the pleading of Aaron (Num 16:1–35).

Clearly, it is not easy for the people to accept that they must wait thirty-seven more years before entering Canaan. Their murmurings are understandable, but not very wise. With the report back from the spies and the example of two easy defeats of the groups that try to infiltrate Canaan, the Israelites are not yet capable of conquering the Promised Land. Best, as God prescribes, to let the weak and untested generation of those over twenty die in those forty years, taking the time to breed two, more numerous generations of new Israelites toughened by life and struggles in the wilderness, all the while creating greater solidarity among the people.

What follows—which involves running when weak, and then fighting when stronger—will test all this out.

The twentieth chapter of Numbers presents a key decision attributed to God—namely, not to let Moses lead his people into the Promised Land. Ostensibly, God denies Moses the leadership in crossing the Jordan and subduing the inhabitants there because Moses "did not believe in me, to sanctify me in the eyes of the people of Israel, therefore you shall not bring this assembly into the land which I have given them" (Num 20:12-13).

What did Moses do to deserve this?

There is a water shortage and Moses and Aaron go before the Lord, who instructs Moses to go a rock and tell it to yield water. Instead, Moses gathers an assembly, strikes the rock twice with his rod, and water comes forth. However, God instructs Moses to verbally command the rock to give water; instead, Moses strikes it. I've heard strange reasons for God's punishment of Moses. One says the rock is really Christ; another says that Moses, by disobeying God, was taking over from God (1 Cor 10:4). My take is far more politically logical, if not widely accepted. God saw Moses, a devoted servant, forget his instructions. What? Of course, he is getting very old. Moses strikes the rock as he had before when water was needed. A forgetful Moses will be far too old to lead the people across the Jordan into a huge protracted battle that will subdue, slaughter, and drive out the existing inhabitants. Joshua, a proven and younger military leader will be better at doing the job. Moses' failure is not really disbelief (lack of belief) but, rather, a memory problem of a declining leader. So, for the rationale of disobedience—it seems really a cover story—Moses is told to eventually retire. Aaron, too, is complicit, and he is even older than his brother. Moses dies (Num 20:10–13; 20:24–29). The best political leaders are those who fit the task.

The wanderings continue. Hoping to travel through the land of the king of Edom, the Israelites turn away after the king denies them permission.

Unlike the king of Edom, who lets the Israelis leave unmolested, the next king does not. The Arad king in the Negeb attacks the Israeli encampment and takes some prisoners. The Israelites, no doubt still suffering the humiliation perpetrated by the king of Edom, plead to God, saying that they will destroy Arad's cities if God helps them. He does, and Arad's cities are destroyed (Num 21:1–3).

This is Israel's first real successful test of strength (the Amalek pushover does not count). The wanderings are a proving ground.

Into the wilderness again, where there is no food or water but lots of complaining to God. In reply, God sends snakes; there is repentance and the bitten survive. This is further proof to the Israelis that God is powerful and with them, even if they sometimes misbehave.

The second big fight also ends in an Israeli victory—this time over Sihon, king of the Amorites, who, like the Arad king, tries to block their way. The Israelites then occupy their cities. Next, the king of Asham gets the same treatment. Victory number three.

By then, the prowess of the people of Israel spreads. Balak, king of Moab, is afraid of the Israelites and seeks an alliance with tribal leader Balaam. Alas, Balaam follows God, refuses, and predicts that Moab and other tribes will fall to Israel (Num 23–24).

So Israel is becoming a militarized nation, relying on war to reach the Promised Land. War, occupation, and revolts will follow them all the days of their lives until Rome does them in, which lasts for the next seventeen centuries. Then, when reconstituted after World War II, the Israelis become—not always on their own initiative—the world's most militarized and militaristic nation, even outpacing number two, the United States. Yes, the "never again" response to the Holocaust still feeds Israel's military political culture not to be victims again. Understandable.

Moses: A Template for Political Leadership

Chapter 25 is an instructive story about Israel remaining ethnically pure and faithful to the one God who brought them out of Egypt.

While dwelling in Shitim, some of the Israelis begin to "play the harlot with the daughters of Moab." Worse still, they bow down to Baal. Moses, obeying God, has the judges slay the chiefs of the wayward. Later, when a man brings a Midianite woman into his family, presumably as his wife, both he and the woman are slain by a priest. This calms God's wrath toward the Israelites (Num 25:1–15), but not towards the Midianites. God tells Moses to smite them (Num 25:16–18).

At this point in our political analysis, it is well to explore a crucial fact about what makes an Israelite. They must be descended from one. The modern Jewish culture determines that a Jew has to have a Jewish mother. However, with so many intermarriages, conversions are fairly common. Professor Michael Walzer writes of conversions, citing Ruth, from the Hebrew Bible book of the same name.[2] Nevertheless, conversions in that book are rare. The Israelites are limited in number, as are modern Jews—a fact that plays a big role when the Israelites face the troops of far bigger empires.

Another census of the tribes is ordered. The people of Israel number 601,330 (Num 26:1–52). However accurate, the people of Israel at that time are a wandering, powerful horde—a force surely to be reckoned with. Laws, internal purges, and wars keep them unified and, with new generations forged by strife, powerful.

God tells Moses that he will die after seeing the Promised Land, but not until Joshua is invested with God's commission of supreme political leadership (Num 27:12–23).

I will pause here to comment on the stature of Israel's leader. Moses has to be regarded as belonging in the pantheon of all historic national leaders. He establishes and keeps his position as the legitimate spokesman of God; convinces Pharaoh to let his people go; quick-times their departure; defeats the pursuing Egyptian forces; solves the people's problems regarding food and water; avoids fighting when weak; unites and toughens the people in their

---

2. Walzer, *In God's Shadow: Politics in the Hebrew Bible*, 5.

Part I—The Hebrew Bible

wanderings; purges dissidents who weaken the nation; establishes laws, ordinances, and ceremonies; appoints essential lieutenants and spies; organizes the structure of his people and government; and leads them to military victories. Yes, the story of Moses is written centuries later, and even with embellishment and selective history, Moses' story still amazes and remains the lighthouse for the Jews and a proof of God's existence for others. He is truly an historic template for political leadership.

Chapter 31 of Numbers tells of Moses ordering war on the Midianites. Again, Israel is victorious, with every enemy male slain, all their flocks booty, and all the women and children captives. All these actions, with the exception of taking the captives, please Moses. He says that the women are the ones who corrupted many Israelis, and orders them to be killed along with all the male children. Only young virgin females can live, presumably as slaves. The booty is divided.

The Israelites wander to fulfill their forty years.

The Lord then tells Moses to order the people to cross over the Jordan, drive out the inhabitants, destroy their works, and settle in the land by allocating land to the various tribes. God tells them to make sure that they do—that if you do not drive out all the inhabitants "they shall trouble you" (Num 33:50–56).

This advice is as worthy today as it was more than two millennia earlier. I and many of Israel's friends urge Israel to establish a Palestinian state; they severely "trouble you." Needless to say, you severely trouble them.

Moses, following God's orders, delineates the boundaries of the Promised Land. So ends Numbers, also called the fourth book of Moses. The Israelis are on the doorstep of the Promised Land.

Last words are given by Moses before the Invasion. Deuteronomy—the last book of Moses—begins with the leader reviewing his efforts, decisions, and his forty years of speaking to all the Israelites (chapters 1, 2, and 3).

In chapter 4, Moses gives statutes and ordinances so that the people may live properly in the Promised Land. He repeats the Ten Commandments and other laws. Moses reminds them that when

Moses: A Template for Political Leadership

they defeat the Hittites, the Girgashites, the Amorites, the Canaanites, the Perizzites, the Hivites, and the Jebusites they "must utterly destroy them; you shall make no covenant with them and show no mercy to them" (Deut 7:1-2). He tells them that God will be with them in absolute victory, will love them, multiply them, and bless them. With God, they will not and cannot fail.

If this is not a great pep talk—more grandiose but in the same genre of a football coach rallying his team before kickoff—nothing is. With Moses' credibility, how can the people of Israel doubt their powers, question the outcome, or even regret the inevitable slaughter that they will impose. No guilty conscience is necessary. They are told that the people whom they will conquer deserve to be slaughtered "because of the wickedness of these nations" (Deut 9:4).

If one considers the inclusive social structure of Israelites, the impossibility of gaining land other than by war, and the cultural legitimacy of war at that time, then slaughtering a whole people—really a genocide—may be seen as necessary. But God is creating a very bad precedent here. Surely today with God, reviewing history and vastly different circumstances, those speaking for the Almighty undoubtedly would give different advice. I'm sure that they now reject his earlier stance, for we already have shown that God can change his mind. We know the horrendous deeds done in the name of God. Is it necessary to mention the brutal Christian Crusades and the Inquisition, the Jewish and Palestinian mutual killings, and the current epidemic of terrorism in the name of Islam?

In the succeeding chapters of Deuteronomy, Moses gives more of the Lord's history lesson and laws, all showing God's power and devotion to the Israelites—on and on. And he says all of this, which must have taken hours, on his 120th birthday (Deut 31:1)!

Then Moses commissions Joshua before the people and tells them that Joshua, who is in God's favor, will lead them to take possession of the land.

Before climbing and dying on Mount Nebo, Moses speaks his own epitaph (Deut 32:1-48) and then gives a very long blessing to the people of Israel, mentioning all the tribes and tribal leaders (Deut 33:1-29).

So ends the life of Israel's founder and lead politician. There is little that a commentator can add to embellish Moses' life's work beyond just recording it.

If the reader is now thinking: Come on, didn't Moses make at least one strategic mistake, do more than the one thing that did not please God, or even have serious doubts about his ultimate success? The story of God and Moses is just too good to be true, really too perfect to be true.

But the reader of the Five Books of Moses, the Torah, must remember that its origins in oral tradition were sifted, shaped, and finally written to glorify and sanctify Israel. There is no need to remind Americans of the George Washington myth or South Africans of the Nelson Mandela myth or the English of the Elizabeth I myth—well, you get the point. All made mistakes but still became icons of leadership. Nations need myths, as I have previously noted.

In fact, there are amazing parallels between the leadership of Moses and that of George Washington.

America's Founding Father ensured his legitimacy by gaining his command via the Continental Congress: he convinces men to flock to his command; flees New York when his forces are too weak; manages an early, easy victory at Trenton over the careless Hessians; toughens his troops at Valley Forge; provides them with food and water; establishes rules and regulations for his forces; appoints lieutenants and spies; preserves his forces in a war of attrition, never risking his forces in a big battle until, with his French allies, he is superior at Yorktown; and finally relinquishes his command (in 1783, he resigns his commission in my hometown of Annapolis, then the U.S. capital) and takes leave of leading America's promised land until it is established in the Constitution. Very familiar, isn't it?

Washington seems to have had a role model.

── CHAPTER 5 ──

War and State Creation

OR SHOULD THIS CHAPTER be titled "God's Military Strategy?" God continues to be portrayed as calling the shots. In the book of Joshua, God or his angel is even around in the guise of the sword-wielding leader (Josh 5:13–15).

War is certainly high politics.

In his now-classic book, *On War*, the notable German military theorist Carl von Clausewitz writes that "war is the continuation of politics by other means."[1] It is a strategy chosen by leaders to bring about a clear-cut conclusion—one in which the leaders hope to gain a complete victory and to impose on the enemy a complete defeat. In its strictest form, there will be no need for compromise (the normal result of a diplomatic resolution of disputes). Compromise involves some giving in order to gain some taking. It has a cost. War does, too. But the calculation favoring combat is that the costs of war are lower than the costs of giving and the gains are of great value. Political theorists call total war a "zero-sum game," where the positive value of the gain by the victor is the same as the negative value of the loss for the loser—hence a zero sum.

Most wars, of course, are not zero-sum. There are wars to provoke diplomacy, such as Egypt's attack across the Suez Canal in 1973 when President Sadat sought to force talks with the Israelis

---

1. von Clausewitz, *On War*.

about normalizing relations and restoring Sinai to Egypt; wars to weaken rivals that are bogged down in foreign conflicts, such as that conducted by the United States in the 1980s by arming the Mujahidin, who were fighting the Soviet occupiers in Afghanistan; wars to repel an invader, which once repelled stops (e.g., the First Persian Gulf War in 1991, which expelled Iraqi forces that attacked and occupied Kuwait); wars to separate territory from the state, such as the U.S. Civil War (1861–65); and wars to overthrow a government, such as the 1789 French Revolution.

The wars of Joshua were zero-sum (the total kind), or close to it. The Israelites would either fully occupy the Promised Land, eliminating its existing residents, or come close to it.

Moses hears God tell him, "But if you leave any previous inhabitants in the Promised Land they will trouble you" (Num 33:55). God tells Moses to eliminate them. Joshua does and doesn't. And trouble they will eventually bring when some are left in Canaan.

The reader is no doubt wondering here what the basis is for this seemingly draconian stricture. It plays a big role throughout the Bible and is clearly relevant today in modern Israel.

Back in Joshua's time, any former inhabitant left will have different gods, not the right God. These people cannot be integrated into Israeli society. This means that they will be second-class citizens at best—or no class at all, probably slaves. They will not be happy, secure, or remotely loyal to the Israelite rulers.

Trouble will likely come when these alien locals among the chosen express resistance to their plight with civil disobedience, sabotage, or revolt. This condition of social instability can be compounded when they seek a foreign patron to help liberate them by waging war against the Israelites. In the same vein, a foreign party hostile to Israel can use the alien community as a fifth column[2] to aid its assault.

In short, aliens are a security threat.

---

2. The label "fifth column" originated during the Spanish Civil War (1936–39), when the Nationalist rebel forces, under Gen. Francisco Franco, counted on supporters in the Republican-controlled territory to aid him and his four columns attacking Madrid. They would be his fifth column.

War and State Creation

Even with more compliant, passive relations between the occupier and occupied, there lurks another danger—one that God is undoubtedly concerned with. Two peoples living together in one land are bound to produce, here and there, friendships, romances, and even marriages. It happens. This could very well lead to agreements to worship the alien gods to cement inter-religious harmony. For a jealous God, this is corruption.

There are two counter-strategies to prevent this: One is to treat the aliens so harshly, physically, using such strict laws to ban relations, that no Israelite would dare mingle with aliens. The other, of course, is to expel the alien residents so that the temptation for corruption simply does not exist.

Alas, there are parallels in the Holy Land today.

There are aliens aplenty when Joshua leads the Israelites across the Jordan. He proves to be a spectacular innovator in military strategies, many of which are familiar to today's readers of more modern military history.

After the death of Moses, God tells Joshua to go over the Jordan into the land that he has given the people, assuring the new leader that if he is strong and courageous, he will have success (Josh 1:1–9).

Joshua sends two spies to Jericho, where they stay in the home of Rahab, a harlot. She keeps their whereabouts a secret from the king, asking only that her family be spared, which is agreed to by the spies (Josh 2:1–14).

Again, spies are used to scope out the enemy's strength and weaknesses, especially fortifications. Intelligence is essential in warfare, and the Israelis are very good at it to this day. In addition to knowing an enemy's capabilities, political leaders need to know an enemy's history and culture. These give clues as to the enemy's intentions—how it is likely to behave. Intelligence can also reveal the personalities at play—where the power lies, as well as their vulnerabilities and strengths.

The spies report to Joshua, saying that the inhabitants are "faint-hearted" (as well they might be) because of the fierce reputation of the Israelites (Josh 2:24). The reputation of the huge nomadic warrior nation has spread. It takes no prisoners. Zero-sum.

Part I—The Hebrew Bible

The book of Joshua numbers Israel's warriors who pass over the Jordan at about 40,000. Chapter 6 tells the familiar story of how the walls of Jericho tumble down. The Lord tells Joshua to take seven priests blowing rams' horns, the ark, and all the people, and march around the city for six days. On the seventh day, after marching around it seven times, Joshua tells the people to shout and "the wall fell down flat." What is likely is this: seven days of intimidation by a superior force had to bring great trepidation to those inside Jericho's walls. In an attempt to escape, some parts of the wall were breached by those trying to escape, allowing the Israelite warriors to enter. In another, more popular, theory, an earthquake shatters the wall. The warriors enter and slaughter all living things except Rahab's family. Manipulating the psychology of the enemy is used to gain victory.

What amounts to genocide may well be necessary to clear the land of inhabitants, but does it make the next target fight harder? It does, to some extent, and the next battle proves it.

Ai is the next target. After spies go to Ai and report that the people of Ai are few and weak, they recommend that only two or three thousand be sent to attack. Surprise! The men of Ai kill about thirty-six Israeli soldiers and chase the rest away, killing more as they retreat.

Joshua pleads with God, questioning his leadership, but God replies that Israel has sinned. Some of the loot from Jericho has been taken for private gain. God demands that the perpetrators and their ill-gotten gains be destroyed. They are (Josh 7:2–26).

Appeased, God orders an attack on Ai, this time with 30,000 fighters. The lesson is learned—"get there first with the most men," as Confederate Civil War General Nathan Bedford Forrest recommends many years later. God tells Joshua to set an ambush. Here's how the plan plays out. After approaching Ai's city with an apparently modest Israeli force, Ai's warriors come out, leaving the city open, no doubt expecting another easy victory. The modest Israeli force, which is the bait, flees and a large, hidden Israeli force takes the city, sets it on fire, and annihilates all the people of Ai, except for the king, who is later hanged (Josh 8:1–29).

War and State Creation

The military strategy here involves maneuvers to give the enemy a false impression—namely, that the Israelite warriors are again weak and outnumbered. Acting upon that impression or assumption brings defeat. Tactics and strategy in war are based on information about the enemy, its relative strength, and its intentions. The ability to manipulate information gives great advantage. In "Operation Mincemeat"—celebrated in books and a feature film about World War II—the British dress a deceased person in an officer's uniform and cause him to be washed up on a Spanish beach with a briefcase fastened to his wrist containing the war plans of the Allies. In the plans, the Allies in 1943 invade German-occupied Europe in Greece (not Sicily, the actual invasion site). The British knew that German spies in Spain would get the information and report it back to Berlin. All goes according to plan. The Germans reinforce the bogus areas, taking them out of position. Other Allied deceptions convince Hitler that the cross-channel operation the next year would be in Pas-de-Calais. Germany puts its top troops in the expected D-Day landing area, not in Normandy, where the Allies successfully land and begin the conquest.

The ambush, a false fleeing to draw the enemy into a vulnerable position, has had a long history ever since it was used by Joshua. For example, the hordes of Genghis Khan used it against mounted European knights to great effect. More recently, the Battle of the Bulge in World War II went that way, not by plan but by German incompetence. The Wehrmacht made a deep bulge in U.S. lines on the assumption that the Americans were weak, covering their front lines in the Ardennes. It anticipated a deep breakthrough, dividing the Allied forces. Once divided, conquered. But the German command discounted the Allied forces on the flanks and so found its troops in a vulnerable position, suffered attrition, and noted its troops' entrance to the bulge nearly closed by Gen. Patton's troops, blocking their retreat. As the skies cleared, Allied airpower slaughtered the Germans. That is the end of Nazi offensive action in the West—a prelude to utter defeat. That the armed forces of Joshua's Israel used it, which could have been its first recorded use, is a tribute to their superior military strategy.

Next, the people of Gibeon, posing as a nomadic, non-Promised-Land people, try to fool Joshua by seeking a deal. Joshua makes peace with them, only to find out later that they are locals. But because he has made peace with them, Joshua spares them and makes them slaves (Josh 9:3–27). Although this can be considered an honorable mistake, it is still a mistake. The error results from a lack of intelligence about the Gibeon tribe.

When the kings of Jerusalem, Hebron, Jarmuth, Lachish, and Eglon—members of an alliance against Israel—learn that Gibeon has defected from that alliance and is now allied with Joshua and the Israelites, they decide to punish Gibeon. The men of Gibeon appeal to Joshua for his help, so Joshua, with God's blessing, leads his forces on an all-night march and a "great slaughter" follows. Many more of the five kings' forces are finished off by the Lord's hailstone attack. All this is aided by extended sunlight until the enemies are mere remnants (Josh 10:1–14). After trapping the five kings in a cave, most of the enemies' remnant forces are wiped out. As he did with the king of Ai, Joshua executes the kings (Josh 10:22–28).

Joshua then destroys the city of Makkedah and kills its king.

The pattern is clear. Joshua employs his full force against enemies one at a time, or one coalition at a time. This always gives him superior numbers. Superior forces assure the odds for success, already favored via superior numbers, by additionally bolstering the morale of those superior forces and crushing the morale of those of the inferior enemy. Libnah is the next victim, then Lachish, then Gezer, then Eglon, then Hebron, and then Debir, thus clearing "the hill country and the Negeb and the lowland and the slopes" (Josh 10:31–43).

Chapters 11 and 12 of the book of Joshua relate scores of further victims. Not one defeat is recorded. In chapters 13 to 23, God divides up the land by tribe.

Joshua, now old, says to the elders, officials, and judges that God fights for Israel and will continue until the land from the Jordan to the great sea in the West is theirs. He reminds them that they must obey the laws that Moses gave them or perish at the

War and State Creation

hand of God. He then reviews their history. The people assure him of their faith in God. Then Joshua dies (Josh 23–24).

If Moses is the great law giver and political leader, then Joshua is the great general and government leader. No great feat—this wandering and conquest is a great feat!—happens without great political and military leaders.

So what does it take to be a good, even great, military leader?

- Full support of the military leader's superior—in Joshua's case, God
- In preparation, an ability to gain allies and to prevent the enemy from gaining them
- Proper training and arming of one's troops
- A clear focus on the enemy, defeating its troops rather than occupying territory
- Knowing the enemy's plans in order to counter them with better plans
- Caring for one's troops, convincing them that victory is likely
- Maintaining popular support for the war, with benefits over costs
- Stamina and good health of the military leader—war is a demanding enterprise

And more than a half millennium before warfare is made a science under the Greeks, Israel develops numerous strategies, now modern strategies: hard basic training in the wilderness; an easy conquest first for morale; espionage for intelligence; the planting of spies; intimidation by demonstrations (as Joshua does around Jericho's walls); terrorism from genocide to induce panic and fear; false fleeing ambushes; local force superiority after segmenting enemies; and—as Gen. Ulysses S. Grant did in the U.S. Civil War—rapid assaults, giving enemies no time to rest, regroup, or coalesce.

These are nothing but first-class military operations. And lest we forget, seeing God as an active player not only boosts morale, it helps ensure success.

Part I—The Hebrew Bible

Yes, history is written by the victor, but the victor makes the history.

The legacy of successful wars in the past is still alive in memory and is reflected today in the enormous military establishments of all major powers. Wars are still celebrated, namely wars that create Israel, Germany, Italy, Vietnam, the United States, and most countries in South America. Wars that protect decent countries from predators, such as Elizabeth I's defense of England from Spain; Tsar Alexander I's defense of Russia from Napoleon; France, Britain, Russia/Soviet Union, and the U.S. defense (however imperfect) against the Kaiser and Hitler; and a similar coalition with China against imperial Japan are also celebrated. So, too, are wars that overthrow corrupt regimes, such as those in France, Mexico, Russia, Cuba, Libya, Iraq, and Afghanistan (here the new regimes are often just as corrupt). As Margaret Mead has written, wars are a well-established human institution.[3]

This legacy and all the military techniques that Joshua and others developed are now in question. The astronomical costs in money, material, and human life of modern war; the looming presence of nuclear weapons; the benefits of economic and political globalization; and the moral repugnance of what is, in reality, an institution of killing and destruction, have created a path, albeit still not paved, toward a less warlike world.

Great impediments to this more benign world still exist, however. As mentioned, victors celebrate great wars, losers hunger for revenge, oppressed peoples struggle for liberation, great military heroes are honored and find themselves available for political office, and all the historic rationales for war exist still.

Not every type of successful politics in the Hebrew Bible, including ethnic cleansing via genocide, is a suitable template for today's politics. Again, Margaret Mead states that any human institution, once learned and established, can be found obsolete and discarded.[4]

Not easy. Some biblical lessons are not for the ages.

3. Mead, "Warfare is Only an Invention – Not a Biological Necessity."
4. Ibid.

— CHAPTER 6 —

Political Power: Glory, Corruption, and Collapse

JUDGES MORPH INTO KINGS in First and Second Samuel, First and Second Kings, and First and Second Chronicles. Saul, David, and Solomon emerge, consolidate executive power, and garner spectacular achievements. The Promised Land expands. Alas, political incompetence arises; Israel and Judah become weak. But sin, falling away from God's statutes, is not the sole reason for their being conquered. That is what the prophets say. They are wrong. Israel is extinguished by the Assyrians. Judah is subjugated and many of its people are taken into exile to Babylon. The reasons for these political failures are clear, even predestined. The Israelites are limited in number by their religious-biological prescription for national membership. They are too few to fend off larger, militaristic empires. Even worse, they divide and fight each other—the ten tribes in Israel versus the two in Judah. They try to remain independent, relying on their illustrious military culture and belief in God's help. Diplomacy is neglected. It is hopeless. When the Persians under Cyrus conquer Babylon, the Jews are allowed to return to the Promised Land, where they rebuild the Temple and become more observant—as if that is the solution to gaining their security. It is not. The Greeks, under Alexander, conquer the Persians and take over Judea. Their rule becomes oppressive, and the Jews revolt under the Maccabees. Judean independence is restored. After a bit longer than four generations, an internal power play erupts. An expanding Roman Empire is invited in to resolve the matter. Judea becomes a protectorate, then a Roman province. The revolt under the Zealots seals the denouement.

Let's trace this political development.

More kings and less God now emerges in the Hebrew Bible. The Almighty appears somewhat frustrated that political leaders take more authority unto themselves. It is a mystery, but the likely conclusion is that God expects his people to gain more dominion, as stated in Genesis, but worries about their capabilities (as well he might). They do make political mistakes.

In First Samuel, a barren Hannah prays to God that if she could bear a son she would "give him to the Lord all the days of his life" (1 Sam 1:1–11). Samuel is born and God speaks to him as he matures. Samuel's words ring true; "none of his words fall to the ground." All Israel recognizes Samuel as a prophet (1 Sam 3:19).

Israel loses a battle with the ever pesky Philistines and then tries combat again. This time, two sons of the priest and prophet Eli (whom God finds wanton) bring the ark of the covenant to the battle. Alas, Israel is defeated, the two sons are slain, and the ark is captured (1 Sam 4:1–11).

This does not bring good fortune to the Philistines. Everywhere they bring the ark, tumors break out among their people. They return the ark in a cart drawn by two milk cows along with gold in the shape of tumors (1 Sam 6:8–21).

Enter Samuel, who tells the people of Israel to put aside foreign gods and calls on God to save his people; the Philistines are defeated in a great battle (1 Sam 7:3–11).

The new role of prophets is established. They hear God and speak in his name. In response to cries from the people who want a king (and with God's seeming approval), Samuel harkens to their voice (1 Sam 8:21–22).

How does this happen?

Chapter 8 relates that an old Samuel makes his sons judges, but they take bribes and are unjust. So the people, unhappy and protesting about the wayward sons, want a king to govern them,

Political Power: Glory, Corruption, and Collapse

just like other nations. With political instability in Israel and Judah, like countries in the same condition, the people usually seek and welcome a strong ruler to set things right. A kingdom must seem appropriate to a settled land—and there are still battles to be fought—needing a strong, upright leader. God, however, sees himself rejected by the people as their king. He tells Samuel to inform the people of the ways of a king, including that a king will use their sons in dubious battle, take their daughters for servants, grab their flocks and harvests, "and you shall be his slaves." This threat doesn't change minds. God then has Samuel tell the people that they will regret their choice to have a king, but that he, not God, will rule (1 Sam 8:1–19).

Later in this chapter, I will briefly analyze and confirm Samuel's (God's) advice about the problems with kings or any absolute rulers. Here, the desire for a kingdom reflects a weak, insecure populace.

Chapters 9 and 10 relate how God picks Saul, a Benjaminite, to be king. He is tall and the most handsome man in the land. He also has the wisdom of a prophet. Samuel anoints him and gives him a book on the rights and duties of a king.

In chapter 11, the Ammonites are poised to conquer Israel. This is Saul's first big test as king. He threatens death to anyone who does not show up to join Samuel and him for battle. They come—300,000 men of Israel and 30,000 from Judah—and in the morning they cut down the Ammonites.

Two political innovations are worth noting.

The first is that Saul, operating on his own, uses his coercive power to ensure that he will muster a strong Army. He, not God (or those who represent God's voice), commands the muster. And second, the victory is *his* victory, thus shifting more power to the monarch and less to God.

One can see a progression. Though miffed, God sees, via his representatives, the necessity of his people becoming more self-reliant, more powerful, and less dependent upon him. Or maybe God has no choice. Saul and the people want more self-reliance and power, and less dependence on God—and they act accordingly. The tension here will not go away. It is historic. The tension

Part I—The Hebrew Bible

between the religious leaders and secular leaders remains to this day—not only in the lands of the three Abrahamic religions but in all lands with significant religious authorities.

Two issues are at play: first, the source of political power—God and his spokespersons or those who hold political office, and second, the proper laws and policies—those from God and his spokesperson or those emanating from those holding political office.

The United States, in the First Amendment, tries to avoid this tension by barring government from making laws respecting the establishment of religion or the free exercise thereof. But even here, questions of school prayer, abortion, contraception, and gay marriage continue to intrude in the political discourse. Since the beginning of the Hebrew Bible, God (and his hearers) and humans (who have their own motives) have at times been at odds. Religion guarantees political conflict, as noted earlier.

In countries where those who represent religious authorities are in power (such as Saudi Arabia, Iran, and even Israel), those in civil society who differ with their religious strictures make their views known. Political conflict results.

Where religious authorities are out of power, as in the United States, it is the religious groups who make their opposing views known. Again, political conflict results.

Where society embraces different religious groups (such as Sunni and Shia in the broader Middle East or Catholics and Protestants in Northern Ireland), conflict between the groups spills over into the government, its staffing, and its policies. Political conflict results here as well.

Countries with little political conflict over religion tend to be those with weak religious authorities, mainly from the lack of a popular base of support and constitutional inhibitions. The Nordic countries are good examples. But even there, the influx of Muslim immigrants is beginning to raise the issue. Political conflict is emerging.

Where there is political conflict over policies and issues, the struggle for supreme political power soon follows.

A rock star emerges.

Political Power: Glory, Corruption, and Collapse

We're still in First Samuel and a battle is pending. Saul's son, Jonathan, goes with his fighters to the Philistine camp. A fight ensues. Saul joins the fray with many Israelites and wins the day.

Saul goes on to battle and defeat the Moabites, Ammonites, Edomites, Jobahites, more Philistines (of course), and the Amalekites (1 Sam 14:1–52). Speaking for God, Samuel orders Saul to kill all the Amalekites, including their flocks. But Saul spares the best of their sheep and oxen, which causes Samuel to regret having made Saul king (1 Sam 15:1–35).

Again, as with Moses, disobedience to God causes a leader to lose his favor with God's spokesman. This time, unlike Moses, the likely cause was not forgetfulness from old age. Rather, it seems to be hubris—ignoring Samuel and arrogantly taking what can be taken. We will deal with the corruptive power of power later in the chapter.

In chapter 16, the Lord instructs Samuel to find a new king in the house of Jesse, the Bethlehemite. After rejecting seven sons of Jesse, Samuel requests the youngest son, who is tending the sheep. He comes. Samuel anoints him. His name is David.

Saul, troubled by Samuel's admonition, seeks a lyre player to soothe him. Yes, it is David. Saul is refreshed and is pleased with his musician.

The Philistines gather again for battle. Out of their camp comes the huge Goliath, heavily armored, challenging an Israelite to a duel. No one comes forward. David, back at his father's house, is sent by Jesse to bring food to his brothers who are under arms with Saul. David arrives and tells Saul that he will fight the Philistine, noting that he has killed a lion and bear while protecting his sheep. Saul agrees to let David fight Goliath.

David rejects armor, takes his slingshot and stones from the creek, and—well, you know the rest of the story. David won, Goliath in two. A wise political-military leader selects the right weapons and strategy to win. David thus becomes a rock star in the eyes of the Israelites. This kindles Saul's jealousy.

It is worth noting again here that military prowess paves the way for political power. Security is Judah's and Israel's prime national interest, so anyone who can provide it becomes a favored leader.

Part I—The Hebrew Bible

Saul's son Jonathan (who loves David) soothes his father's enmity against David. It does not last. With Jonathan's help, David flees Saul, gathers supporters, defeats more Philistines (they are slow learners and seem to be poor warriors as well), and rejects the chance to kill the pursuing king. David confronts Saul, saying, convincingly, that he is a loyal subject. They are reconciled. Saul acknowledges that David will someday become king.

This, too, does not last. Fearful, David and his men become refugees and actually reside with the Philistines. As is their habit, the Philistines prepare to attack Saul. David is willing to help his refugee providers, but the Philistine commanders do not trust him. He is sent back to his exile home. Saul, without his best warrior-leader, loses the battle and falls upon his sword (1 Sam 31:1–6).

In the meantime, Samuel also dies.

So goes the story of one of history's most famous political rivalries, where the one in power fears the one who will likely be his premature successor. Jealousy and paranoia come into play. Saul is especially bothered by the popular song at the time:

"Saul has slain his thousands, And David his ten thousands" (1 Sam 18:7).

Because of his enmity towards David, Saul has lost his key military commander, whose absence results in defeat and death.

Even though David makes no move to replace Saul, the king loses self-control and also loses God's (Samuel's) favor. Wisely, David bides his time, undoubtedly knowing that, because of his erratic, irrational behavior, Saul is bound to come a cropper. Good politicians sense that when events are favorable without efforts expended on their part, it is best to let events take their course. There is an old political saw that says, "If your enemy is digging himself into a hole, let him continue digging."

David is a good politician. But he develops faults, as we shall see.

The story continues in Second Samuel.

David mourns the death of Saul and Saul's son, Jonathan, and for the people of Israel. "How the mighty have fallen" (2 Sam 1:27).

Political Power: Glory, Corruption, and Collapse

David asks the Lord whether he should go to a city in Judah. He hears a response: Go to Hebron. There, the people anoint him king over the house of Judah. In Israel, the commander of Saul's army, Abner, puts the dead king's son, Ishbosheth, on the throne. At Gibeon, David's forces defeat the forces of Israel. The plot twists. Abner makes love to one of Saul's concubines. Ishbosheth objects, and Abner defects and goes to David, after rallying the people of Israel in David's favor. They reconcile. Abner, however, is murdered by one of David's men in a blood-feud issue. David and all the people weep for Abner (2 Sam 3:1-39).

Two captains in Ishbosheth's army murder the king and take his head to David. As David killed the person who helped Saul fall on his sword, he does the same with the two captains (2 Sam 4:1-12).

All the tribal leaders of Israel come to David, who makes a covenant with them at Hebron and is made king. He rules for 33 years (2 Sam 5:1-5).

Although David is not complicit with Saul's or Ishbosheth's deaths, their demise—one after a losing battle and the other murdered—foretells political selection as a deadly game. Good governance has an established method of selecting leaders. Here, hereditary succession is ruptured.

David seizes Jerusalem and calls it the City of David. Both "become greater and greater, for the Lord, the God of hosts, was with him" (2 Sam 5:9-10). David also takes many wives and concubines, producing a large number of sons and daughters.

After being assured by God, David defeats the ever-warlike but ill-fated Philistines. He goes on to expand Israel, defeating many tribes and nations, including the Syrians, who are occupied and bring tribute (2 Sam 8:1-8). War is so common and expected that Second Samuel notes: "In the spring of the year, the time when kings go forth to battle . . . " (2 Sam 11:1). Israel is an aggressive warrior nation, then as it is now. David is clearly feeling his supreme political power.

And power corrupts, of course. If a political ruler wants something badly enough and has the means to get it (even if it is illegal or unethical), the temptation to get it can be overwhelming. So it was with David, who sees the naked and beautiful Bathsheba from his rooftop and lusts after her. After seducing her and causing her to become pregnant, he orders her husband to be put in the most dangerous front line in an upcoming battle. He is, of course, killed. David takes Bathsheba as a wife. This "displeases the Lord" (2 Sam 11:27). The prophet Nathan, speaking for the Lord, tells David that he is forgiven but that Bathsheba's child shall die. Bathsheba's next child lives; he is named Solomon (2 Sam 12:24).

The Absalom conspiracy against David begins when Amnon, a son of David, rapes his sister, Tamar. Another son, Absalom, then kills Amnon but flees from David, fearing retribution. After three years, David allows Absalom to return to Jerusalem and is reconciled. This is a mistake, for Absalom covets the throne and tells the men of Israel that he will bring them justice. Unlike the complacent David, he is glad-handed politician. Absalom's following grows large; the men are tired of David's wars. Alarmed, David flees with a large force. Absalom pursues them, but David's troops attack and defeat the Israeli forces under Absalom. Contrary to David's instructions, they kill Absalom. David grieves (2 Sam 13–18).

Many wars with the Philistines follow, but David's men eventually take him out of harm's way, for he is getting old (2 Sam 21:15–17). David praises the Lord, his rock, who delivers him from danger and gives him love. It is a long praise poem (2 Sam 22, 23:1–7). They are the last words of David.

First Kings begins with David's decline and incapacitation. Adonijah, one of David's sons, attempts, with the support of military commander Joab, to become king. But David's military supporters and the prophet Nathan go to Bathsheba, telling her to go to David to remind him of his pledge to make Solomon king and get his confirmation. David, then aware of Adonijah's attempted coup, agrees to have Solomon anointed king (1 Kgs 1:1–40).

David dies. Here again is the fundamental problem—there is no established process for making a king. David has so many children that it becomes, by default, his job to select the next king. But what if he is totally incapacitated or dies suddenly?

Political Power: Glory, Corruption, and Collapse

Solomon soon kills his brother, Adonijah, and his mentor, Joab. Solomon appoints his own administration, priests, and army commanders (1 Kgs 2:13-35).

In his first political policy move, Solomon creates an alliance with Egypt by marrying Pharaoh's daughter (1 Kgs 3:1-3).

This marriage probably reveals two political situations. The first is that Solomon is worried about Egyptian aggression. War is habitual then. The alliance is to head it off. The second, after a rocky path to his kingship, the king needs space to focus on domestic politics—namely, solidifying his status and mapping out an agenda. Proof of the last situation comes soon. He praises God and offers sacrifices. God comes to Solomon in a dream and says: "What shall I give you?" The king replies that he is inexperienced and not learned, and therefore requests "an understanding mind to govern thy people." God grants Solomon's request approvingly, because he did not ask for riches, long life, or victory over his enemies. God then adds riches and honor and long life if he keeps God's statutes (1 Kgs 3:3-14).

Solomon proves his wisdom in the case of two women who claim to be the mother of the same baby and appeal to his judgment. After testing both women by ordering that the baby be cut in two, the real mother, of course, objects. He then awards the baby to its rightful mother. Solomon basks in popularity. He appoints more officials. The population of Israel and Judah grows; all are happy from the Euphrates to the land of the Philistines to the Egyptian border.

Building a house for the Lord is Solomon's first domestic policy. A deal with King Hiram of Tyre brings him cedar and cyprus of Lebanon and quarried stone. Solomon mobilizes 130,000 workers for the project of constructing the magnificent Temple, as described in all of chapter 6.

Again, two points are worth making. To say that there is soon full employment in Israel and Judah would be an understatement. In addition, the magnificence that results has to fill every heart with pride and joy. King Solomon cements his rule. As modern political leaders cut ribbons and make speeches to open a building,

Solomon does the same in front of the assembled people. A feast follows.

Solomon makes all the non-Israelites slaves, leaving the men of the country to become soldiers. With the aid of ally King Hiram of Tyre, he builds and dispatches ships of trade (1 Kgs 9:20–28). King Solomon is at his zenith.

It is not to last, however.

Solomon violates the covenant, which is really the Israelite constitution. One key provision of the covenant commands: "You shall not enter marriage with [foreign women], neither shall they with you, for surely they will turn away your heart after their gods." Solomon marries an Egyptian and has Moabite, Ammonite, Edomite, Sidonian, and Hittite lovers—700 wives, who are princesses, and 300 concubines, all told, and he sacrifices to their gods (1 Kgs 11:1–8).

Needless to write, the Lord is angry. But for the sake of Solomon's father, David, God says that he will "tear the kingdom from you" in your son's rule, leaving him with only one tribe (1 Kgs 11:9–13).

It bears repeating that the Hebrews are to be one people, united, worshipping the one true God, not procreating with foreigners or worshipping their gods. There is no melting pot in Israel or Judah. During constant wars, the one people will fight and die to protect each other, not foreigners. It is a cardinal statute.

This explains why, after Solomon dies, his son Rehoboam is destined to rule with a heavy hand. He employs forced labor and increases taxes beyond even the onerous yoke of Solomon. He provokes a popular revolt. The new king is left with only Judah, the capital of which is in Jerusalem. Rebel leader Jeroboam rules Israel, the capital of which is in Samaria, and he, too, sins by worshipping gods of his own making. With the Israelites divided, the two kings fight. A weakened king Rehoboam suffers a plundering by the king of Egypt. Here, First Kings tells readers to read the book of Chronicles of the Kings of Judah for the history of the rivalry. After Rehoboam dies, his wayward son, Abijam, takes

Political Power: Glory, Corruption, and Collapse

the throne; later, his son Asa ascends the throne—finally, a righteous ruler (1 Kgs 14, 15:1–15).

Wars between Judah and Israel rage for years, with Israel's kings killed one after another. Sin, doing evil in the sight of the Lord, is given as the reason that so many die while Asa lives on.

Enter the prophet Elijah. He bests the priests of Baal in a contest to make a burnt offering burn. His fame spreads; he anoints Jehu king of Israel, then Ahab, who defeats the king of Syria and puts his army to flight. The Syrians attack again in the spring, but are again put to flight. It is downhill for Ahab from then on.

Ahab's wife, Jezebel, murders a vineyard owner in order to give her husband the property he covets. Not good.

There follows a series of struggles, even wars, between the kings of Judah and Israel. Great internal strife also afflicts both kingdoms. That the kings do not do well in the sight of God should surprise no one. Kings are programmed to be corrupt. They have too much power, revel in it, and have as one of their top aims the keeping of it by suppressing any opposition. Good kings, such as Asa and his son Jehoshaphat, are stark exceptions. But even with these two there is not much virtue, or, in Jehoshaphat's case, intelligence. These are not glory days for Judah or Israel.

Elijah hears God condemning Ahab and Jezebel. Ahab repents and God repents on his behalf, but not entirely. Ahab's son will be the target of God's wrath.

After three years of no wars between them, Asa's son Jehoshaphat—the new king of Judah—and Ahab make peace and contemplate attacking the king of Syria. They consult many prophets, who urge war. One prophet, Micaiah, dissents, and Ahab has him thrown into prison with only bread and water to eat and drink (1 Kgs 22:1—28). The kings attack Syria.

Evil and stupidity then mix. Ahab tells Jehoshaphat to go into battle wearing his kingly robes, while he will battle in a disguise. Incredibly, Jehoshaphat agrees to the plan, and so becomes the singular target of the Syrian king. In battle, Jehoshaphat tells his attackers that he is not king of Israel and gets away. Ahab is not so fortunate—he dies.

Jehoram is the next to rule in Judah; Ahaziah rules in Israel. They worship Baal.

In Second Kings, the prophet Elijah foretells Ahaziah's death, who, of course, dies (2 Kgs 1:1–17). There follows chapter after chapter about the sinful leaders of Israel and Judah; only King Jehu rules well—mainly by slaughtering the priests of Baal. Rule is little better in Judah, but it is still better. King Hezekiah destroys false idols and altars and, with the help of the prophet Isaiah, counters military encroachments from Assyria. His successor, King Josiah, renews the devotion to God's laws and celebrates the long-neglected Passover ceremony. Unfortunately, bad rulers follow these good ones.

Alas, Assyria then conquers Israel and takes the captured people back to Assyria with them (2 Kgs 17:1–6). Once scattered, the ten tribes of Israel are lost to history.

Later, the King of Babylon conquers Judah, destroys the Temple, and takes the captured people to exile in Babylon (2 Kgs 24, 25).

The loss of God's favor, directly attributed to the sins of their rulers (their "abominations") is meant to explain both conquests and highlights the necessity of following God's laws and statues. God is not blamed for these tragedies afflicting his people. Well, sin they might, but the major sin is political. Even Israel and Judah combined are at a disadvantage in numbers when facing powerful empires. Divided they fall. Here again, we see the theme of people taking more power and God seemingly powerless to stop bad rule and behavior. Biologically limited in size, Judea's rulers mistakenly rely on combat, neglecting diplomacy and disaffecting their people.

Both books of Chronicles trace the familiar stories set in First and Second Kings. The genealogy of the Hebrews occupies the first nine chapters in First Chronicles. The ending of the Second Chronicles has a twist. Babylon is conquered by Persia. The prophet Jeremiah foretells God's promise of relief from exile. The Lord then stirs up the spirit of King Cyrus, who says: "The Lord, the God of heaven, has given me all the kingdoms of the earth, and he has charged me to build him a house at Jerusalem, which is in Judah. Whoever is among you all his people, may the Lord his God be with him. Let him go up" (2 Chr 36:23).

Political Power: Glory, Corruption, and Collapse

The book of Ezra begins with the very words that end Second Chronicles. Cyrus returns all the loot taken from Jerusalem by Nebuchadnezzar. All the captives return to Jerusalem (Ezra 1, 2:1–2). There are 42,360 Jews among them and 7,500 servants and singers (Ezra 2:64–67).

After making burnt offerings to the God of Israel, they go about rebuilding the Temple with the support of Cyrus and Darius, his successor. Passover is celebrated upon the completion of the Temple. Ezra, a priest and scribe, is appointed by the next Persian king, Artaxerxes, to hold authority in Jerusalem.

All is well until officials in the city note that the people of Israel and even priests have taken local non-Jews for wives. This faithlessness appalls Ezra, who sees the repeat of the very sins that he believes caused captivity and shame in the past. He gathers the men and tells them to "separate yourselves from the people of this land and from foreign wives." And they do (Ezra 9, 10).

Our political analysis of the Hebrew Bible ends with Judah part of the new Persian Empire when its emperor Cyrus allows the Jews to return to their homeland. There they restore the Temple and religious observances. Thus begins the Second Temple era in Jewish history.

In 331 BCE (before the common era), Alexander the Great conquers Darius III, the last Persian king. This brings Judah under the control of Greek empires. Judah, now called Judea, comes under the domain of the Seleucid kingdom, a Hellenistic monarchy, in 198 BCE. It does not go well. The Seleucids desecrate the Temple. In 167 BCE, the Maccabean-led revolt recovers Judean control after three years of bitter warfare. This is celebrated in Hanukkah, commemorating the miracle of extended oil light in the recaptured Temple. The descendants of Judas of Maccabee, the leader of the revolt, rule Judea from 143 to 40 BCE. This Hasmonean dynasty breaks down in civil and religious conflict when two brothers vie for supreme power. Both factions appeal for help from Rome.

This is a big mistake. Roman general Pompey, while concluding his conquest of the Seleucid kingdom in Syria, intervenes in 63 BCE, in effect putting Judea under the hegemony of Rome.

Part I—The Hebrew Bible

Pompey has a non-Hasmonean prince named Antipater made governor under the Hasmonean king. Antipater becomes number one with support from his patrons—first Pompey, then Julius Caesar. His son, Herod, is appointed a regional governor.

After Caesar's assassination, a Hasmonean faction assassinates Antipater. With Cleopatra's help, Herod flees to Rome. There he asks and receives the aid of Mark Antony and the young Octavian (later Caesar Augustus) to be named King of Judea. The Roman Senate ratifies the choice in 40 BCE.

Herod the Great becomes one of the world's premier builders. He refurbishes the Temple and constructs the port of Caesarea, royal palaces, and many public buildings that grace Judea. Rome, when it can find loyal and effective local rulers, rules through them. The modern British Empire in its heyday does the same. It is called indirect rule. The political theory behind it is clear. Foreign subjects are more likely to remain more quiescent if their local rulers are from their own community. It also reduces the need for occupational personnel and saves money by employing low-wage locals. Herod rules with an iron fist but brings great prosperity to Judea. He dies in 4 BCE. His son, Archelaus, rules Judea; a better description would note that he misrules the kingdom. Roman Emperor Caesar Augustus replaces him with a procurator, a military governor. Judea becomes a Roman province. Pontius Pilate serves in the position from 26 to 36 CE.

In short, powerful foreign forces confront Israel and Judah. A combination over time of dependence on a foreign patron, misrule, unmanageable internal political conflicts, an over-reliance on military tradition, ideological breakdown, and weakness resulting from an exclusive, biologically limited, and divided population produces monumental political failure. Flawed humans, not God, are in command.

Clearly, new politics with a new strategy are called for. Such a conclusion occurs to one who sees himself as God's son—an anointed one assigned to correct the political situation by changing the religious one.

Part II

The Christian Bible

THE CHRISTIAN BIBLE ALSO includes the Hebrew Bible, what Christians call the "Old Testament"—a name obviously not favored by Jews. The Hebrew Bible is included for a number of reasons. The Hebrew God is the same God as the Christian God. Jesus is a Jew. Christians believe that the Hebrew Bible foretells the coming of Jesus as their and the world's messiah. In addition, it gives Christianity an ancient heritage, a pedigree much admired in ancient times as it is today. That Rome largely respected Judaism as an ancient religion made the Christian attachment to the older faith efficacious. Otherwise, the Jesus cult would be considered new and a likely threat to Roman imperium and would suffer even greater persecution.

All this denotes the transition for Christians from the Old to the New Testament.

There is another reason, one not understood for the transition from the Hebrew Bible to the Christian. That is a major subject of this book.

Our political analysis of the Hebrew Bible ends with Judea as part of the Roman Empire, soon to be extinguished when Jews unsuccessfully revolt. The reader must keep in mind that religion (church) and government (state) are one. When a religion loses its state and is subordinated to another government, the people representing that religion will strive to throw off that yoke. This explains why the Jews, against all odds, revolted (twice) against Rome as they had against their former Greek masters. Not only was Rome not their state, it had a bad habit of desecrating the Temple.

The Hebrew Bible describes a monumental political failure, as the last chapter analyzed. Judaism as the basis for the Hebrew state does not succeed. Even more to the point, the Hebrew state as the basis of Judaism fails. The record is clear. There are major flaws in the Jewish state's concept and practice. The prophets attribute the conquest and occupation of Israel and Judah to the chosen people falling away from God and his statutes. Nonsense. The real reasons are political.

A brief review: Basing a state on an exclusive religion—one that limits the community to a biologically derived body of people, and a relatively small one at that—existing in a part of the world of competing, militant empires is, well, a big mistake. In addition, Israel and Judah fight against each other and are extinguished separately. If the Hebrews want to remain small and exclusive, their political strategy has to focus on good government and diplomacy, making alliances with the dominant empire, whether Babylon, Persia, Greek, or Rome. But becoming a client state of those more powerful was anathema to the Jews. Second, they are too elitist, too much top-down control of privilege, wealth, and power. The masses remain weak and receptive to reform. Third, they unwisely rely on their military prowess and tradition—a glorious one up until the time of Solomon. Except for the Maccabean/Hasmonean interlude, their military record becomes dismal. And as Jesus predicts, resorting to combat would put an end to Judea. This happens in the Zealot revolt of 66–70 CE, resulting in the destruction of the Temple and the start of a major diaspora of the Jews. Judea becomes Palestine, even more of a Roman province.

Yes, Judea becomes a failed state.

This does not please Jesus. He creates a Jewish-to-Gentile movement to redress the adverse political situation. Christianity centered on Jesus eventually subverts and becomes the state religion of the Roman Empire, thus expanding God's domain. God's people are again politically secure. In addition, the diaspora spreads Jewish culture worldwide. A case can be made that it is the main ingredient of virtually all cultures today—in poetry; science; history; architecture; rituals; and, most decidedly, in monotheism. And it should be noted that most Christians believe that Jews remain God's chosen people; otherwise, why include the Hebrew Bible in their own?

Jesus and those speaking for God resolve to shift political strategy. There is the hope that God would directly intervene to destroy all evil authority—an apocalypse—and install God's kingdom with a coming-again Jesus as king. An associated strategy would also be put in place. God's chosen people have to expand and become a major political force among the Gentiles. Not all Jews agree, however, and their numbers devoted to Jesus fall. Nevertheless, Christianity would be that movement sweeping up adherents in the Roman Empire. It was a bottom-up strategy. As it happened, that would be the strategy that worked. Rome eventually decides it needs Christianity and makes it the state religion in 391 CE.

Ever since the first conquest of Judah by the Babylonians and all the subsequent conquests of the Promised Land, Jews nurtured the hope of a messiah. He would have two tasks. Because the decline, persecution, and captivity of the Jews are attributed to their falling away from God and his statutes, the messiah would restore adherence to the laws. He would also, in the mold of David, deliver the nation from its oppressor. God would be with him and aid him in these tasks. All the major and minor prophets stressed this apocalyptic theme, going back to the Babylonian captivity.

For example, the great eighth century BCE prophet Isaiah provides two passages that seem to presage an apocalyptic messiah and what Christians believe foretell the coming of Jesus.

"Therefore the Lord himself will give you a sign. Behold, a young woman shall conceive and bear a son, and shall call his name Immanuel. He shall eat curds and honey when he knows how to refuse the evil and choose the good" (Isa 7:14–15).

Part II—The Christian Bible

Or this passage, made familiar in Handel's *Messiah*: "For us a child is born, to us a son is given; and the government shall be upon his shoulder, and his name will be called 'Wonderful Counselor, Mighty God, Everlasting Father, Prince of Peace.' Of the increase of his government and of peace there will be no end" (Isa 9:6–7).

Various minor prophets all have apocalyptic themes— Haggai (Hag 2:1–10, 20–23), Zephaniah (Zeph 3:14–20), Zechariah (Zech 14:1–20), and Malachi (Mal 3:6–17, 4:1–5).

There is much in the Gospels that portrays Jesus as an apocalyptic messiah—that is, as an anointed politician who will rule God's kingdom. I will reinforce this portrayal using his own words. He also acts like a politician and, just as importantly, is treated by the Jewish and Roman authorities as one.

Jesus is a politician on a campaign.

I suspect that this role has been downgraded, even missed, out of respect for his religious role in bringing a new covenant from God. For some it appears to denigrate and transcend Judaism. More to the point, the name and role of a politician has a not-too-admired status in many countries, including my own. As a political analyst and practitioner, I strongly disagree. Leaders are absolutely essential to bringing peace, security, well-being, and purpose to any community. Where would Americans be without George Washington, Abraham Lincoln, Franklin D. Roosevelt, Dwight Eisenhower, and the like? Where would the Jews be without Moses, David, and David Ben-Gurion?

And where would Christians be without Jesus?

Of course, observant Jews find this Christian notion nonsense. The Christian God is their God. Christianity, therefore, is a Jewish sect (offshoot) which mistakenly believes that Jesus is the Christ (the messiah) and the Son of God. Jews see themselves still as the chosen people, with Christians as self-selected. They may agree that Jews become the vehicle for the spread of Christianity and that Christians facilitate, both by their persecution and eventual aid, the creation of modern Israel. They may also acknowledge that the diaspora spreads historic aspects of the Jewish culture worldwide—an unparalleled contribution to humanity. But God's

Part II—The Christian Bible

plan failing with the Jews? No. If it appears that way, such a conclusion is a mistake.

This retort has not stopped the Christian movement. Both Abrahamic religions live—sometimes in heavy conflict, sometimes in harmony. Both endure and thrive.

Alas, for Christians the hope of God's apocalypse does not come to be. Jesus' apocalyptic vision becomes a metaphor presaging a larger kingdom of God.

The seeds of the real and enduring strategy—the creation and spread of a large, potentially powerful Christian movement—then come into play. For that, Paul and all the subsequent apostles do the planting. They must do so via the Roman Empire, and we note characteristics of that imperium that facilitate that expansion.

Unlike the Hebrew Bible, in which God and his agents are largely politically in charge, God and his agent Jesus are *not* politically in charge in the Christian Bible, although they are political founding fathers. They are working under alien political powers as they create a new, popular political-religious movement to redress the political failure presented in the Hebrew Bible. This is politics creating religion so that both Jews and their offshoot sect may thrive as an expansion of God's chosen people.

— CHAPTER 7 —

Jesus the Politician

LET US IMAGINE WHAT Jesus thought of the world around him when he began his mission.

He sees the Jewish leaders; Herod, who murdered his mentor and friend John the Baptist; and the Pharisees and Sadducees as incompetent political toadies of the pagan Roman rulers. They are not the legitimate rulers of the Jews. He sees the Jewish masses as exploited, suffering, and in need of a messiah (an anointed one)— not a violent revolutionary but one to lead a new political-religious movement. He sees his message, representing God, as non-violent, humane, and, most of all, promising salvation and therefore capable of mobilizing not only Jews, although they are the first to be recruited as missionaries, but also eventually Gentiles. God's people need to expand and live in a peaceable kingdom. Jesus remembers that Isaiah and Jeremiah prophesy that the Hebrew God would become the God of all. He sees the Roman Empire as the target, an organization that can facilitate the expansion of a new Judaism and eventually harbor it. With God's help, he is willing to stake his life on it. He will use his death and resurrection to trigger the completion of his mission that begins a whole new chapter in political, human, and religious history.

The Nicene Creed, established by the Council in Nicaea called by the Roman Emperor Constantine in 325 CE and modified by a council in 381 CE, is a proper frame for analyzing Jesus the politician. The Council was called to put an end to all the splits in Christian doctrine and organization and thus to create an orthodox faith. The Roman leader wanted religious unity in the Empire—one that would bolster imperial authority. Emperor Theodosius I, in 391 CE, would make Christianity the state religion. The Creed presents many of the political themes about Jesus that will be explored in the Four Gospels. It reads:

> We believe in one God, the Father, the Almighty, maker of heaven and earth, of all that is, seen and unseen.
>
> We believe in one Lord, Jesus Christ, the only Son of God, eternally begotten of the Father, God from God, light from light, true God from true God, begotten, not made, of one Being with the Father; through him all things were made. For us and for our salvation he came down from heaven, was incarnate of the Holy Spirit and the Virgin Mary and became truly human. For our sake he was crucified under Pontius Pilate; he suffered death and was buried. On the third day he rose again in accordance with the Scriptures; he ascended into heaven and is seated at the right hand of the Father. He will come again in glory to judge the living and the dead, and his kingdom will have no end.
>
> We believe in the Holy Spirit, the Lord, the giver of life, who proceeds from the Father [and the Son], who with the Father and the Son is worshiped and glorified, who has spoken through the prophets. We believe in one holy catholic and apostolic Church. We acknowledge one baptism for the forgiveness of sins. We look for the resurrection of the dead, and the life of the world to come. Amen.

First, Jesus the politician will be revealed, as the Creed posits. Jesus is extremely powerful, as one with God and also as the creator of the earth. Most importantly, "He will come again to judge the living and the dead, and his kingdom will have no end." This is the apocalypse, the sweeping away of sin and evil, and the establishment of a new kingdom under Jesus as judge and king. The political message is clear.

Next, the process whereby Jesus builds his followers—what today's political analysts would call his political base of support—will be made clear in exploring "for our sake" his service to the poor, the ill, and the outcasts. He heals, even raises the dead, and his fame spreads. Just as important, Jesus spares no reluctance to verbally chastise the Jewish elite, but takes no overt political action until his last week in Jerusalem. These efforts and, as the Creed states, his promise of eternal life constitute his appeal to the masses. He is building a new community envisioning new leadership. This is Jesus and his followers taking on the role of political subversives; he is building a new movement that will eventually be politically official when it merges with the Roman Empire.

Finally, the Creed notes that Pilate has him killed. The Roman procurator considers Jesus a political rabble-rouser and subversive. He is a threat to his rule and to Rome. If authorities see and treat him as a politician, they undoubtedly must have good reason to do so.

The Apocalyptic Messiah

The belief that Jesus would come again soon after his crucifixion is a belief which he himself had. With God sweeping away all evil and sinful authorities, Jesus, then, after judging the living and the dead, would rule as king in a peaceable, loving, and eternal kingdom.

There is evidence, as we will show in chapter 8, that from Acts and letters and books in the Christian Bible some apostles—Paul, in particular—share this belief and use it to recruit Christians.

Needless to write, this belief in Jesus coming again to rule has been cast in doubt, certainly its early appearance. However, it is still in the Nicene Creed—the orthodox statement of fundamental beliefs of many Christian denominations and sects to this day.

So if the timing was wrong, it is still anticipated, however distant.

That it is on the Christian back burner and not talked about much should not deter us from exploring the evidence for it and its political implications. After all, God and Jesus ruling the world are—if you will forgive the pun—high politics.

Here is the evidence:

We begin by laying the foundation for God's and Jesus' apocalypse.

Jesus believes and portrays himself as the Son of man, God's son, and the messiah, although his reference to himself as the messiah is rare and indirect.

Many of his followers, especially his disciples, express a similar image of Jesus. This can be seen in Mark 8:29-30 while he is questioning his disciples. "And he asked them, 'But who do you say that I am?' Peter answered him, 'You are the Christ.' And he charged them to tell no one about him."

Later in Mark, before his crucifixion but after the crowd from the chief priests and scribes seize Jesus, he is brought before these religious authorities and questioned. Witnesses say that they heard Jesus say he will destroy the Temple and build another in three days. "And the high priest stood up in the midst, and asked Jesus, 'Have you no answer to make? What is it these men testify against you?' But he was silent and made no answer. Again the high priest asked him, 'Are you the Christ, the Son of the Blessed?' And Jesus said, 'I am; and you will see the Son of man sitting at the right hand of Power, and coming with the clouds of heaven'" (Mark 14:60-63). This is one of the rare times that Jesus, engineering his trial and crucifixion, confesses his person. Usually—and this is the case here—Jesus has others identify him.

This set my political mind to recall what all wise political leaders do. They rarely, if ever, tell voters or legislators how great they are. They never say: I am all-knowing and wise; do what I want. Instead, they gain stature and credibility from testimonials from others remarking how great and what wonderful political leaders they are. Why? Self-puffing has no credibility at all. It is unseemly, self-centered, and culturally off. Laudatory comments by respected others, on the other hand, do convey credentials and stature. In addition, Jesus probably does not want to infuriate the chief priests and scribes just yet with evidence that he is the Christ (messiah). They would take that as blasphemy and confront him. Later, as noted and quoted above from Mark 14, that confrontation is inevitable—and, for Jesus, necessary. No reason remains to hide it. He wants to make known right then who he is. He is, as noted above, planning his own crucifixion.

Jesus acts like a seasoned politician.

However Jesus times his messiah (anointed one) message, it is not difficult to convey that, with all this power and powerful backing, God would do what is expected. That is, sweeping away corrupt, sinful local leaders and Rome and installing the kingdom of God under Jesus makes sense.

Jesus is quoted in the Gospels of Mark, Matthew, and Luke in this apocalyptic vein. The Gospel of John, coming decades after the other three synoptic (similar outline) Gospels, does not do so. John has a far different focus. His has been called the poetic Gospel. It also may be that whoever wrote John, after considering that the apocalypse hasn't happened, simply left it out of his story.

Mark, the earliest Gospel, begins: "The beginning of the gospel of Jesus Christ, the Son of God. As it is written in Isaiah the prophet, 'Behold, I send my messenger before thy face, who shall prepare the way; the voice of one crying in the wilderness: Prepare the way of the Lord, make his path straight . . . '" (Mark 1:1–3).

Later, Jesus is quoted after gathering the multitude with his disciples: "'For whoever is ashamed of me and my words in this adulterous and sinful generation, of him will the Son of man also be ashamed, when he comes in the glory of his Father with the holy angels. And he said to them, 'Truly, I say to you, there are some standing here who will not taste before they see the kingdom of God come with power'" (Mark 8:38—9:1).

Matthew has it this way. "These twelve Jesus sent out, charging them, 'Go nowhere among the Gentiles, and enter no town of the Samaritans, but go rather to the lost sheep of the house of Israel. And preach as you go, saying, 'The kingdom of heaven is at hand'" (Matt 10:5–7). This is followed by: " . . . and you will be hated by all for my name's sake. When they persecute you in one town, flee to the next; for truly I say to you, you will not have gone through all the towns of Israel, before the Son of man comes" (Matt 10:22–23).

Luke waxes long on this apocalyptic theme.

In chapter 21, Jesus speaks to his disciples, telling them that in days to come "when there shall not be left here one stone upon another that will not be thrown down." He continues, saying, "the end will not be at once." There first will be wars, earthquakes, famines, pestilences, and your own persecutions, but you will be saved. Furthermore, "Jerusalem will be trodden down by the Gentiles, until the times of the Gentiles are fulfilled." Next, there will be signs, "for the powers of the heavens will be shaken. And then they will see the Son of man coming in a cloud with power and great glory. Now, when these things begin to take place, look up and raise your hands, because your redemption is drawing near" (Luke 21:26–28).

Even more explicit is this passage in Luke of Jesus' charge to his disciples at the Passover feast before being handed over to the authorities. "You are those who have continued with me in my trials; as my Father appointed a kingdom for me, so do I appoint you that you may eat and drink at my table in my kingdom, and sit on the thrones judging the twelve tribes of Israel" (Luke 22:28–30).

Whenever all three synoptic Gospels present the same theme—a very political theme—this is likely an authentic expression of Jesus that flows from the oral tradition and whatever writings are available. No wonder that early Christians, especially Paul, whose letters precede the Gospels by decades, nurture an apocalyptic happening. This powerful message serves to recruit early Christians and is one that still attracts some fundamentalist Christians today. It would make sense to be on the right side of the great apocalyptic divide soon, for it might come any day.

If one expects to be king, one needs to seek and nurture loyal subjects.

JESUS THE POLITICIAN

Jesus and His Disciples Recruit Followers

Let us turn now to the political strategy of expanding God's people—the recruitment of members for what in the late first century, early second CE becomes referred to as Christianity.

Jesus does not organize his church or appoint its officials but instead targets creating believers and supporters for his Jewish core group. His whole ministry reflects this primary mission, which is analogous to a political campaign. He aims center on transforming the religious-political world. Through Jesus, God expands his people's numbers, but not by God choosing them as the Lord did with the Hebrews. Instead, God has his agents "become fishers of men," as Jesus tells his fishermen disciples in Mark 1:17. Jesus' supporters, taking the bait, choose Jesus.

The Roman Empire serves to facilitate this new Godly task. A new universal domain depends upon a near universal existing domain at the height of its reach and power.

This is bottom-up politics as well as bottom-up religion.

First to be considered is the credibility and legitimacy of the Christian message of devotion to Jesus as the Son of God. This will focus on the miracles and the resurrection; both, if believed, prove that such power can only be a genuine confirmation of the message.

We will then explore the appeal of the Christian message of elevating the self-worth and value of the individual man and woman; of guiding proper, ethical behavior; and, most importantly, of personal salvation. This will be juxtaposed with the contrary Roman culture—one with little appeal to what we today call the common man (and woman) and those who speak and act in their name.

Finally, in the same line of thought, the criticism of Jesus aimed at ruling authorities—mainly Jewish, rarely Roman—serves to recruit those suffering or neglected under their rule.

The synoptic Gospels tell of thirty-two miracles that Jesus performs, and his very clever way of telling their benefactors not to say who perpetrates them. Jesus, of course, knows that there will be violations, adding to their mystery and influence. Secrets revealed have higher impact, inflating the reputation of the subject.

Part II—The Christian Bible

The Gospels have Jesus healing early in his mission.

This from Matthew: "And he went about all Galilee, teaching in their synagogues and preaching the gospel of the kingdom and healing every disease and every infirmity among the people. So his fame spread throughout all Syria, and they brought him all the sick—those afflicted with various diseases and pains, demoniacs, epileptics, and paralytics—and he healed them. And great crowds followed him from Galilee and the Decapolis and Jerusalem and Judea and from beyond the Jordan" (Matt 4:23–25).

Mark reports the same event. A man "with an unclean spirit" confronts Jesus in a Capernaum synagogue, saying, "'What have you to do with us, Jesus of Nazareth? Have you come to destroy us? I know who you are, the Holy One of God.' But Jesus rebuked him, saying, 'Be silent, and come out of him!' And the unclean spirit, convulsing him and crying out with a loud voice, came out of him. And they were all amazed, so they questioned among themselves, saying, 'What is this? A new teaching! With authority he commands even the unclean spirits, and they obey him.' And at once his fame spread everywhere throughout all the surrounding region of Galilee" (Mark 1:24–29).

Luke, in virtually the same language, repeats the story (Luke 4:31–38).

Many healings follow. Jesus raises the dead, with Lazarus being the most famous case.

These are testimonials to the power of Jesus to command, and to command representing God's authority. Connect the healing to his message of the kingdom of God and personal salvation and that message widely resonates. No wonder his fame spreads, exactly as Jesus intends.

All this is crowned by his resurrection from the dead. Then and since, the resurrection of Jesus is central to the Christian belief. Without it, as historian Bart D. Ehrman noted in his book, Jesus would not be remembered but, rather, would be just another forgotten political criminal put to death by the Romans for preaching nonsense.[1] Theologically and historically, nothing confirms for

---

1. Ehrman, *How Jesus Became God; The Exaltation of a Jewish Preacher*

Jesus the Politician

Christians more than this third-day event that Jesus is the Messiah and the Son of God.

Someone totally unaware of the story and hearing it for the first time most assuredly would find it bizarre. Arranging a fake human sacrifice to drive home a point? Please! Yet it is a powerful lesson about God because it is so implausible. God's authority can do wonders!

The promise of salvation, of life everlasting in heaven where there are "many dwelling places," has brought millions to Christ and even has convinced an untold number to lay down their lives in obedience to this promise. His resurrection offers proof of the forgiveness of sins and the promise of eternal life, of salvation for all of the faithful. God and all people can be reconciled.

The focus of his message and mission is clear. He does not curry the favor of the Jewish elite or the Sadducees, Pharisees, or Herodians. He seeks the masses, the poor, the ill, and the outcasts, such as tax collectors and harlots. The Pharisees, in particular, complain and chastise Jesus for eating with these outcasts (Matt 9:10–13).

Jesus also feeds the multitudes with his miracle of loaves and fishes (Matt 14:26–21).

Perhaps nothing extols his appeal to the multitudes more than what is called his Sermon on the Mount (Matt 5–7). The Beatitudes sum up that appeal to those who hear them there. Similar stories of the event are found in Matthew, Mark, and Luke. Matthew 5:3–14 says:

> Blessed are the poor in spirit, for theirs is the kingdom of heaven.
>
> Blessed are those who mourn, for they shall be comforted.
>
> Blessed are the meek, for they shall inherit the earth.
>
> Blessed are those who hunger for righteousness, for they shall be satisfied.
>
> Blessed are the merciful, for they shall obtain mercy.

---

from Galilee, 6.

Blessed are the pure in heart, for they shall see God.

Blessed are the peacemakers, for they shall be called the sons of God.

Blessed are those who are persecuted for righteousness sake, for theirs is the kingdom of heaven.

Blessed are you when men revile you and persecute you and utter all kinds of evil against you falsely on my account. Rejoice and be glad, for your reward will be great in heaven, for so men persecuted the prophets who were before you.

You are the salt of the earth; but if salt has lost its taste, how shall its saltiness be restored? It is no longer good for anything except to be thrown out and trodden under foot by men.

You are the light of the world. A city on a hill cannot be hid. Nor do men light a lamp and put it under a bushel, but on a stand, and it gives light to all in the house. Let your light so shine before men, that they may see your good works and give glory to your Father who is in heaven.

Here is a slightly different version from Luke (6:20–31):

Blessed are you poor, for yours is the kingdom of God.

Blessed are you that hunger now, for you shall be satisfied.

Blessed are you that weep now, for you shall laugh.

Blessed are you when men hate you and when they exclude you and revile you, and cast out your name as evil, on account of the Son of man!

Rejoice in that day, and leap for joy, for behold, your reward is great in heaven; for so their fathers did to the prophets.

But woe to you that are rich, for you have received your consolation.

Woe to you that are full now, for you shall hunger.

Jesus the Politician

> Woe to you, when all men speak well of you, for so their fathers did to the false prophets.

The poor, the meek, the persecuted, and the reviled are not part of the elite. Yet, Jesus extols blessings for the masses and tells them that theirs is the kingdom of heaven. Though not the elite, they are the multitude. In his many parables, Jesus preaches proper behavior, broadcasting an ethical culture far different from that of the Jewish elite and certainly different from that of the Roman occupiers. Besides the popular appeal of salvation and of eternal life, the promise of joy from a moral life has proven over the ages to have great attraction. Buddha preached it to great effect in gaining adherents. People find great personal satisfaction in loving, caring for, comforting, and protecting fellow humans. They feel good because they are good. Jesus, and later the apostles, wisely focus on this recruiting tactic in their teaching. In his story of the good Samaritan—the lower caste traveler who rescues and cares for a mugging victim—Jesus portrays this good neighbor as actually pleased, even happy, to be of compassionate service (Luke 10:25–37). His reward is the happy issue of his efforts.

A case can be made that Jesus often preaches about freedom—something in short supply in Roman Palestine. As analyzed in chapter 4, God and Moses see the need for an extensive, somewhat harsh set of laws to be imposed over unruly, uncivilized Israelites. Jesus, by being less concerned with strict law enforcement, opens the way for more choice. This is illustrated when he is asked by a Pharisee lawyer: "Teacher, which is the great commandment in the law?" In answering, he condenses the laws to: "You should love the Lord your God with all your heart, and with all your soul, and with all your mind. This is the great and first commandment. And a second is like it. You shall love your neighbor as yourself" (Matt 22:36–40, Mark 12:28–31). Or when he heals on the Sabbath and is chastised, Jesus replies that to do good and save a life is more important (Mark 3:1–6). Similarly, when his hungry disciples harvest grain to eat, which the Pharisees say is against the law, Jesus answers, "I desire mercy, and not sacrifice" (Matt 12:1–8).

This leads to another wonderful recruiting tactic.

Imagine illiterate, oppressed, subsistence lower-class Jews in his time. Here comes someone who tells parables and stories. These are designed to make them think and to figure lessons out for themselves. Clearly, Jesus is giving his audience great respect—in effect, telling them that they are worthy and capable of good judgment. This elevates their status. And as every good politician knows, this tactic brings votes.

Also note that Jesus deals with multitudes, great crowds. Here the twelve disciples play an essential role. In modern political campaigns they are called the "advance men" (and women)—preparing the venue, disseminating publicity about their candidate's events, and recruiting an audience. They also promote the legacy of the leader after he is out of office. In short, they are modern disciples and apostles. The twelve truly are advance men and missionaries.

Jesus' disdain for the ruling authorities, both religious and political, is also designed to curry favor from the multitude. He is preaching a version of equality. All people (perhaps not the rich) have a chance to reside in God's heaven. The cultures in Judea and Rome are segmented by class and birth—patricians over plebeians in Rome and the equivalent in Judea. Jesus' individualism also contrasts with the collectivist culture in both places. There is also his emphasis on pacifism, turning the other cheek—something not respected by Roman or even Judean elites.

Jesus Becomes a Political Threat to Rome

The growing popularity of the Jesus movement is seen as a political threat by the chief priests and scribes and, more decisively, by Pilate. They correctly perceive Jesus as a political actor. Ironically, by treating him as one, they make him and his movement a powerful political force.

Jesus rightly masks his political role until the end. He does not want to come to the attention of Pilate until he enters Jerusalem and performs his concluding miracle. Rarely does he mention either Herod or the Romans. Doing so would dilute and sully his message of faith, ethics, and salvation. He knows full well what

Herod did to John the Baptist after he became too critical of Rome's puppet leader.

Privately, he tells his disciples to beware of the Pharisees and Herod. He does so after the disciples tell Jesus that they forgot to bring bread in their missionary travels. "And he cautioned them, saying, 'Take heed, beware of the leaven of the Pharisees and the leaven of Herod'" (Mark 8:15).

Most famously, when the Pharisees try to bait Jesus in order to get him in trouble with the Roman rulers, Jesus cleverly deflects them, as told in the following story.

> Then the Pharisees went and took counsel how to entangle him in his talk. And they sent their disciples to him, along with the Herodians, saying, 'Teacher, we know you are true, and teach the way of God truthfully, and care for no man; for you do not regard the position of men. Tell us, then, what you think. Is it lawful to pay taxes to Caesar, or not?' But Jesus, aware of their malice, said, 'Why put me to the test, you hypocrites? Show me the money for the tax.' And they brought him a coin. And Jesus said to them, 'Whose likeness and inscription in this?' They said, 'Caesar's.' Then he said to them, 'Render therefore to Caesar the things that are Caesar's, and to God the things that are God's.' When they heard it, they marveled; and they left him and went away. (Matt 22:15-22)

Yes, it is a marvelous deflection, thus avoiding the trap and a premature challenge. He really doesn't answer the question. To answer "yes," he would infuriate the Pharisees and other devout Jews, while to answer "no" would incite Pilate to quash this rebel. Either answer would provoke his premature seizure. Jesus still had work to do—mainly instructing his disciples at the Last Supper and in the Garden of Gethsemane.

The Last Supper, in particular, has Jesus instructing his disciples—and eventually all believers—in a ceremony with great religious-political implications. As told in Matt 26:26-28: "Now when they were eating, Jesus took bread, and blessed and broke it, and gave it to his disciples and said, 'Take, eat; this is my body.' And he took a cup, and when he had given thanks he gave it to them, saying, 'Drink of it, all of you; for this is my blood of the covenant, which is poured out for many for the forgiveness of sins.'" And Paul adds, in 1 Cor 11:23-26: "Do this for the remembrance of me" after each instruction. The Eucharist is a ceremony wisely composed to keep Jesus alive in memory for all time. People eat and drink daily. The daily remembrance serves to keep the faith alive and is the reason it is used by all Christian churches in their services, starting with those in Paul's time. Saying Christian grace before meals serves the same function of keeping the faith and his movement alive.

Two other functions of the Eucharist (with functions defined as "intended effects") are equally important in building the movement and sustaining it.

By taking in the symbolic body and blood of Christ, Jesus resides inside that person as a companion, protector, inspirer, and comforter. This ritual instills the faith and installs a commitment to the movement. This is a highly beneficial function.

So is the second. Eating and drinking is, at best, a social affair—an event signifying friendship, family, community, and, in an ultimate sense, mutual love. What better way is there to establish a group—one that builds solidarity with each member participating in one symbolic body? Except for Judas the betrayer, the other eleven disciples attending the Last Supper cemented their commitment to build the movement—implicitly political—even if they did not recognize it as an immediate objective, pointing the way to all their future endeavors on behalf of it.

Jesus' strategy changes in the final week that he plans his crucifixion and resurrection.

He begins by arranging a loud and public entrance to Jerusalem. To fulfill Hebrew prophecy, he has the disciples get a colt for him to ride and then recruit and instruct a crowd of supporters. They wave palms, line the path with cloaks, and shout, "Hosanna! Blessed is he who comes in the name of the Lord! Blessed be the kingdom of our father David that is coming! Hosanna in the highest!" (Mark 11:1–10).

Jesus the Politician

This demonstration, with its explicit political overtones—the kingdom of our father David that is coming—no doubt catches the attention of the chief priests and scribes as well as the Roman authorities.

There is a repeat performance by Jesus the next day. He enters the temple as Passover approaches. He needs the Judean authorities to want him out of the way via the condemnation by Pilate. The story is similar in all the synoptic Gospels. Here it is as told in Mark.

> And they came to Jerusalem. And he entered the temple and began to drive out those who sold and those who bought in the temple, and he overturned the tables of the money-changers and the seats of those who sold pigeons; and he would not allow any one to carry anything through the temple. And he taught, and said to them, 'Is it not written, 'My house shall be called a house of prayer for all the nations?' But you have made it a den of robbers.' And the chief priests and scribes heard it and sought a way to destroy him; for they feared him, because all the multitude was astonished at his teaching. (Mark 11:15–18)

As I understand it, to buy a sacrificial animal for Passover, the Jews have to convert blasphemous Roman coins for Temple coins, hence the money-changers. They and the chief priests undoubtedly take a cut and are not appreciated. So Jesus makes a popular point, hence the fear. But most importantly, this gets the chief priests and scribes to act the way Jesus designs.

There is a telling passage in John regarding how this comes about. The chief priests are primed to get rid of Jesus. Following the raising of Lazarus and after the Pharisees find out about the miracle, they gather in council.

> What are we to do? For this man performs many signs. If we let him go on thus, everyone will believe in him, and the Romans will come and destroy both our holy place and our nation. But one of them, Caiaphas, who was the high priest that year, said to them, 'You know nothing at all; you do not understand that it is expedient for you that

one man should die for the people, and that the whole nation should not perish' . . . So from that day on they took counsel how to put him to death. (John 11:47–53)

Whether exactly factual in language or not, the passage clearly indicates the belief at that time that the behavior of Jesus has enormous political implications—according to the chief priest—involving both Judea and Rome.

The triumphal entrance and the money-changer episode give the chief priests and scribes the immediate rationale for their task.

The motive of Judas for turning in Jesus has been long debated. Is he a Zealot disappointed in the pacifism of Jesus? Although author Reza Aslan asserts in his popular book that Jesus is a warrior leader,[2] he fails completely in making the case. Nowhere in the Bible does Jesus call for a revolt or is he organizing, leading, and arming fighters. Citing Matt 10:34–36 is hardly proof that Jesus is a warrior Zealot. It reads: "Do not think that I have come to bring peace on earth; I have not come to bring peace, but a sword. For I have come to set a man against his father, and a daughter against her mother, and a daughter-in-law against her mother-in-law; and a man's foes will be those of his own household." In this context, Jesus is telling his disciples that in following him they and other believers would face hostility, even within their own families, and so must prepare for persecution, the sword. In fact, Jesus, in taking on the role of a warrior Zealot, would guarantee that Rome would crush his movement before it becomes firmly established, as Rome tried in a real Zealot revolt—but too late—three decades after his death. Does Judas favor the thirty pieces of silver (not likely, given that he disposes of them when he realizes the deadly consequences of his betrayal)? For whatever motive, he does the deed and Jesus is brought before the chief priests and scribes.

The synoptic Gospels all have Caiaphas, priests, and scribes questioning Jesus, asking if he is the Christ. Jesus answers in Mark: "I am; and you will see the Son of man sitting at the right hand of Power" (Mark 14:62). In Matthew: "You have said so. But I tell you,

---

2. Aslan, *Zealot: The Life and Times of Jesus of Nazareth*.

Jesus the Politician

hereafter you will see the Son of man seated at right hand of Power, and coming in the clouds of heaven" (Matt 26:64). In Luke: "If I tell you, you will not believe; and if I ask you, you will not answer. But from now on the Son of man shall be seated at the right hand of the power of God" (Luke 22:67-69). John does not report his confrontation with Caiaphas; he says only that the chief priest sent him to Pilate (John 18:28).

Blasphemy is the verdict. This clearly is a cover for the political motive that Caiaphas spoke of to the others.

Pilate makes no secret of the political necessity for executing Jesus, although he hides his responsibility for it with dexterity.

Pilate does not condemn him for blasphemy. He finds no fault in Jesus for this charge brought by the chief priests with the elders and scribes—a charge that is an issue for the Jews but not for Rome. Pilate has a different issue for Jesus, and one that is very political.

The version of the trial from Mark:

The first words from Pilate confirm the Roman governor's concern. "Are you the King of the Jews?" Jesus answers: "You have said so" (Mark 15:2).

Pilate says no more to Jesus, but goes out to the crowd that the chief priests had organized and, as was the tradition of Passover, offers to release a prisoner. "Do you want me to release for you the King of the Jews?" Pilates asks them. The crowd, as instructed by the chief priests and scribes, calls for the release of Barabbas and shouts, "Crucify him." So Pilate, "wishing to satisfy the crowd, releases Barabbas for them and, having scourged Jesus, he delivers him to be crucified" (Mark 15:6-15).

Pilate, knowing Jesus' growing number of followers and his claim to be king of the Jews, sees him as a rising political threat. Already he stirs up the people, creates turmoil in the Temple, and defies Rome by his failure to deny his political ambition. Pilate has no choice. Time to put a stop to this problem and be done with it.

If he only knew!

But Pilate is a politician, too. And he transfers blame for his decision onto the Jewish elite by acceding to their shouted demand. Doing so satisfies his Jewish puppet clients and deflects the anger of Jesus' followers from Rome for the execution. Pilate probably now believes that his action restores calm, ends threats, and makes Roman rule more secure.

In Matthew, undoubtedly copying Mark (the earliest Gospel), Pilate asks the same question and Jesus gives the same answer. And the episode with the crowd is very similar, but with a controversial addition. "So when Pilate saw that he was gaining nothing, but rather that a riot was beginning, he took water and washed his hands before the crowd, saying, 'I am innocent of this man's blood; see to it yourselves.' And all the people answered, 'His blood be upon us and on our children'" (Matt 27:11–25).

Only Matthew has this final phrase—one that has unjustly been used by Christian anti-Semites to condemn Jews as "Christ killers."

Rome killed Christ.

Luke contains a very lengthy account of the trial and condemnation. There are some new and very political charges brought by the chief priests and scribes. "And they began to accuse him saying, 'We found this man perverting the nation, and forbidding us to give tribute to Caesar, and saying that he himself is Christ the king'" (Luke 23:2). Then Pilate asks the same question as in Mark and Matthew. "You have said so," answers Jesus. Pilate says he finds "no crime in this man." This stirs up Jesus' accusers, adding: "He stirs up the people, teaching throughout all Judea, from Galilee even to this place." This gets Pilate's attention and, finding out that Jesus is from Galilee, sends him off to Herod (who is in the city for Passover). After mocking him, Herod sends Jesus back to Pilate, who disingenuously says that he will release him. Then follows the familiar denouement, with the Romans placing an inscription over his cross: "This is the King of the Jews" (Luke 23:1–38).

John also has a long account, with Jesus more talkative, but the process and the outcome are the same (John 18:19–40, 19:1–17).

Pilate cares little for theological disputes among the Jews; he only desires that they remain sequestered. However, in this case they did not, and, worst of all, they have major political implications to the rule of Pilate and Rome.

Jesus the Politician

The resurrection of Jesus must have been seen then as it is now—that Rome could not kill Jesus or his movement. Jesus is the victor; he and his movement will prevail, presaging the demise of pagan Rome to the advent of a Christian Rome.

With his resurrection and appearances before first the women and then the disciples and others, Jesus accomplishes his mission, his campaign—one that he plans to be the first act of a longer drama. Not only is it seen in the liturgy as proof of the promise of eternal life, it is as well an indication of an eventual triumph over pagan Rome.

And of course it was and is.

The disciples, besides being advance men, are also proselytizers for the new faith. It begins among Jews who are the vehicle to soon branch out to include more and more Gentiles. They follow Jesus' admonition. Here it is in Matt 28:16–20: "The eleven disciples went to Galilee, to the mountain to which Jesus had directed them. When they saw him, they worshipped him; but some doubted. And Jesus came and said to them, 'All authority in heaven and on earth has been given to me. Go therefore and make disciples of all nations, baptizing them in the name of the Father and of the Son and of the Holy Spirit, and teaching them to obey everything that I have commanded you. And remember, I am with you always, to the end of the age.'" In effect, God now reveals his universal pedigree, the God of all. The apostle Paul is accorded a prime role in the enterprise.

They all function in the Roman Empire. It is a political system, a huge interconnected domain, and a guarded territory that both facilitates the spread of Christianity and creates its greatest challenges. Many Christians rightly believe that God had to await a new political climate for Jesus to come and be able to spread his faith worldwide.

To trace the biblical accounts of Christianity's growth and its eventual political subversion of the Roman Empire, we first explore the apostles' impact on the Empire's culture as they create Christians.

Part II—The Christian Bible

Some conclusions: When planning to write this book, I was frequently asked why I would write a book about the Bible as politics. That is not its purpose. Well, then I explain that in a major way it is about politics. Understanding the connection between what are called the Old Testament and the New Testament is essentially political. Jesus is portrayed as addressing the political mistakes in the first with the political correctives in the second. Religious strictures in the Hebrew Bible play a part in its political mistakes, and politics in the Christian Bible play a key part in creating a new religion.

In addition, it is, as we have shown, also a powerful set of political stories, and understanding them as such brings more understanding of the Bible as part of history. History is dominated by politics. And politics has been, if not dominated by the Bible, rather powerfully influenced by it, so here we are.

The Bible, wrongly applied, has influenced some horrendous behavior. Think of the crusades, inquisitions, tortures, witch hunts, and devastating religious wars.

Then again, think of its far more lasting and positive applications. It guided many political reforms, such as the end of slavery, the liberation of women and minorities, the end to draconian punishments and child labor laws, movements inhibiting senseless wars, the reform of government constitutions, and the elimination of colonial occupations.

We could cite the careers of leaders inspired by and guided by the Bible. Nelson Mandela and Martin Luther King, Jr. are the most recent examples.

I will briefly explore the amazing parallels between Mahatma Gandhi's political movement and the movement of Jesus just analyzed. Jesus creates a political template.

Mohandas Gandhi is born in India in 1869, marries at 13 (arranged but successful), becomes a good student, and goes to London at 19 to study law at University College. He is called to the bar in 1889. Gandhi moves to South Africa four years later and becomes a leader of the abused immigrant Indians. Following his return to India in 1915, he:

Jesus the Politician

- Stands up for the pariah caste, whom he calls "Harijans" (Children of God).
- Calls for home rule
- Adopts a strategy of nonviolence
- Recruits disciples under the banner of the Indian National Congress
- Performs symbolic acts to gain legitimacy, including spinning his own clothes and leading a procession to make salt, thus challenging the salt tax
- Gains millions of supporters and adherents to his mission
- Challenges British rule, with nonviolent labor strikes and hunger strikes (Britain promises dominion status after World War II.)
- Advocates national unity among Hindus, Sikhs, and Muslims, but finally accepts the partition of the country when it becomes inevitable
- Is martyred in 1948 by a Hindu extremist opposed to partition
- Has others who revere him change his name to "Mahatma" (Great Soul) Gandhi, his nation's savior

The life of Jesus (and the writings of Tolstoy, which Gandhi had also read extensively) clearly provides guidance for Gandhi's successful strategies in creating a new nation with its own state. What works in an earlier political context is worth emulating.

CHAPTER 8

The Subversion of Rome

Isaiah, Jeremiah, and certainly Jesus believe that the Hebrew God will become the God of all, thus creating the new religious-political movement. It will be subversive of Rome, because it will undermine the existing order, resulting in pagan Rome becoming Christian Rome.

Paul, especially, builds the movement via his teaching an appealing gospel, providing leadership with wise advice on internal church matters and on their relations with authorities, and in managing the coordination of the entire movement. The political strategy for growing the Christian movement and subverting Rome is outlined by Paul in his letter to the Romans. It is absolutely brilliant.

Paul may be the most important in the quest; however, Peter becomes the first leading apostle in the recruiting effort.

The Acts of the Apostles begins with post-resurrection Jesus coming to his disciples, telling them to remain in Jerusalem "to be baptized with the Holy Spirit." They ask, "Lord, will you at this time restore the kingdom to Israel? He says to them, 'It is not for you to know times or seasons which the Father has fixed by his own authority. But you shall receive power when the Holy Spirit has come upon you and you shall be my witnesses in Jerusalem and in all Judea and Samaria and to the end of the earth'" (Acts 1:6–8).

The Subversion of Rome

Besides Jesus' charge to Peter and the other disciples to expand God's people, there is the promise of the apocalypse, where the evil power of Rome will be swept away by God and the Son of man to establish God's kingdom that now includes Gentile believers along with Jews. Thus, going beyond the Jews to gain new believers is reaffirmed. The Roman Empire facilitates it.

Pax Romana is an essential condition in the growth of this increasingly political socio-religious movement. Rome builds an extensive road network and shipping infrastructure, establishes law and order for personal security, creates a monetary system that facilitates the exchange of goods and services, and extends the Greek and Latin languages to a vast area. These all interconnect scores of societies—clans, tribes, and nations. And they certainly facilitate proselytizing in a large arena in terms of safe travel, common literacy, and letter messaging.

This becomes fertile ground for a more appealing religion aimed at an ambitious political objective.

Roman gods—there are lots of them—are similar to those of the Greeks, but have different names. These gods will make trouble if not appeased by worship and sacrifices. They control the sea, crops, and cities. Obeisance to them, therefore, serves to avoid being abused. The gods, furthermore, are intimate allies of the Roman state. As with the Jews, there is no separation of church and state. This makes worshipping the gods and state via obedience, sacrifice, and applause a means to avoid abuse and trouble. This elite culture puts costs on the common people for disobedience—the plebeians, non-citizens, and slaves, and even some wayward patricians.

There is not much love of humanity from the gods or from the state. Obedience to the power elite holds sway. Nor is there much personal relationship between the individual Roman and the gods of the state. Prayer, if that can exist, must consist of keeping the gods from doing harm.

This, indeed, creates fertile ground for the Christian message, which offers a loving and protective God who, through Jesus, promises eternal salvation. Salvation, available to all—slaves,

107

women, outcasts, soldiers, laborers, and the poor—has great appeal to the masses.

Believers, steadfast in their faith in their own resurrection, can better endure persecution trusting in that hope. And this endurance becomes testimony to the power of their God, further spurring the spread of Christianity. It bursts upon the scene throughout the Empire, at first heavily Jewish but increasingly including Gentiles.

The confirmation that all the Christian proselytizing is political comes from the solid fact that there is no belief anywhere of the separation of church and state. Thus, to create a dominant church requires that a dominant state be its partner and protector. Rome is the obvious target.

Some readers may argue that just because it turned out that way doesn't mean that capturing Rome for Christianity was intended from the beginning of the movement. However, if the entire process of building Christianity—mobilizing the masses and even more and more of the elite—points in that direction, one can assume that a conscious effort is being made to attain that goal. After all, Christianity, with its Judaic roots, is believed by some Christians to be the only true religion and it should be officially recognized as such.

Upon receiving the Holy Spirit, Acts relates, Peter and the rest of the disciples preach salvation, the gospel of a resurrected Jesus Christ. Peter heals a lame man and many others. Thousands believe, are baptized, and contribute money (Acts 2, 3, and 4). The angry Jewish authorities arrest Peter and the other apostles (missionaries) and throw them into prison, "but an angel of the Lord opened the prison doors and brought them out," telling them to preach in the Temple. Despite being warned not to speak in the name of Jesus, they continue to do so. The number of believers multiplies (Acts 5).

Luke, the author of Acts, then tells of the martyrdom of Steven. Saul, an anti-Jesus Pharisee, is present at Steven's stoning. He rounds up believers (Acts 6, 7, and 8) and goes to the high priest to get a letter to the synagogue in Damascus so that he can seize more believers there. On the way, Jesus comes to him (Acts 9:1-9). Blinded, Saul hears Jesus tell him "to carry his name to the Gentiles and kings and sons of Israel" (Acts 9:15). He recovers in Damascus, preaches, avoids a plot by angry Jews to kill him, goes to Jerusalem, is protected by Barnabas, is accepted, and is saved by the brethren when the Hellenists seek to kill him (Acts 9:16-31).

Acts then relates the missionary work of Peter, who raises a man from the dead, converts a Gentile centurion and his friends, and convinces the other apostles that God has cleansed Gentiles for conversion. These apostles then preach the word in Phoenicia and Cyprus (only to Jews), and in Antioch, where Greeks become believers. Peter is again jailed and again miraculously is freed by an angel (Acts 12:1-11).

The rest of Acts focuses somewhat exclusively on Saul (soon to become Paul). There are clear indications that Luke becomes close to Paul in his later travels. But Paul's first companion is Barnabas. They have similar missionary experiences. They go to Antioch (where believers are called Christians for the first time), Cyprus, Antioch of Pisidia, Iconium, and Lystra; return to Antioch, where they appoint elders for every church; and then continue to Philippi in Macedonia with Silas and Luke, to Thessalonica, and to Beroea. In every instance, they convert Gentiles and make believers of Jews. This infuriates some Jewish leaders, who threaten them; they even stone Paul, who is left for dead in Lystra. Paul and his companion flee, but not before spreading the word and creating churches. Their work is dangerous; Paul's courage gains admirers and believers. He ends up in Athens, where he preaches, creates interest among the philosophy-loving Greeks, and identifies God to them as their "unknown god." He gains believers. Then Paul goes to nearby Corinth, where he stays for a year and a half (Acts 11-17).

Paul's next mission adds a new dimension to his effort to create a diverse and large Christian community. Women, too, become apostles. Paul goes to Ephesus in Syria with Priscilla and Aquila. He then leaves for Antioch, going "from place to place through the region of Galatia and Phrygia, strengthening all the disciples" (Acts 18:23). Back in Ephesus, Priscilla and Aquila instruct the apostle Apollos of Alexandria in the true gospel after he makes mistakes with Christians there (Acts 18:24–28). Women in Roman culture, while not oppressed, clearly have a more than modest, approved role. Christianity can be seen as a liberation from seclusion and subordination. Women are increasingly converted, and they effectively play a part in spreading the faith to men as well as women.

Paul, back in Ephesus, preaches in the synagogue for three months, kindles opposition as well as believers, and takes his message to a meeting hall for another three years (Acts 19:11–17).

The hostility of Jewish leaders toward Peter and Paul has been noted. It intensifies. At first, when the apostles speak of Jesus as the messiah of the Jews, that message is adamantly rejected. Later, when Christian churches and elders are created, it is clear that this is a departure from traditional Judaism, a breach of faith. Christianity is separate and is seen by Jewish leaders as a threat to Jewish identity and their status. A split becomes more evident. Paul becomes a serious target. This soon changes Paul's life and itinerary.

Paul stays in Asia, after sending helpers Timothy and Erastus to Macedonia. He runs into trouble with Jewish silversmiths, who produce images of the Roman god Artemis. They object to Paul's apparent disdain for Artemis, which hurts their business. The silversmiths drag the disciples to the theater, seeking blood, but the town clerk, fearing Roman intervention, dismisses the crowd (Acts 19:23–41). Paul goes to Macedonia, then to Greece, and, of course, flees after learning of a Jewish plot on his life. Then, with his helpers and Luke, Paul leaves for Troas, goes next to Assos, and then sails to Mitylene, Chios, Samos, and Miletus, where he rallies the elders of the church (Acts 19, 20:28). Still with Luke and others, he sails to Tyre, Ptolemais, and Caesarea, where he is told that the Romans want him in Jerusalem. He goes there, meets Jesus' brother James, and is seized by Jews from Asia, who accuse him of teaching against the laws of Moses. About to be assaulted and killed, Paul is rescued by a tribune and his soldiers and is arrested. Paul is a disturber of the Roman peace—something that Roman authorities are programmed to squash. He tells the Romans his story without effect, and is about to be scourged. Saying that he is a

The Subversion of Rome

Roman citizen stops the proceedings (Acts 21, 22). Paul is put before a Jewish council (probably the Sanhedrin) and he assures them that he is a Pharisee. This produces no positive effect. A plot to kill him has the tribune send Paul to Felix, the governor in Caesarea, where his accusers can make their case in a proper setting. There is a trial without judgment. Felix wants a bribe and keeps Paul in prison for two years to get it (Acts 23, 24). At that point, Felix is replaced as governor by Porcius Festus, who conducts a new trial. Paul, as a Roman citizen, appeals to Caesar for judgment. Festus decides, "To Caesar you shall go." But before dismissing him, the governor has Paul appear before Agrippa, the king and area Jewish leader. Paul defends himself, telling his Jewish bona fides, his Damascus revelation, and Jesus' gospel. Surprisingly, Agrippa finds no fault with him, probably knowing that, since Paul had appealed to Caesar, he would have to go to Rome and would no longer be a problem (Acts 25, 26). Best to get rid of this troublemaker.

Paul sails to Rome with Luke, who, in describing the journey, uses "we," indicating his companionship with the apostle. A violent tempest at sea causes the ship captain—afraid of crashing on a sandbar (or rocks)—to anchor off an unfamiliar land.[1] In the morning, after cutting the anchor cables, the ship crashes on a sandy shoal, sinks, and, as Paul has predicted to the crew, all 276 on board make it to shore (Acts 27). The survivors experience warm hospitality, especially Paul. He heals the father of Publius, the Roman chief of the island. Paul heals others, preaches, and converts, and, after three months there, sails to Rome.

Luke ends the book of Acts by writing that Paul speaks there for two years, welcoming visitors and teaching (Acts 27, 28).

Before analyzing Paul's letters in his quest to build a mass political-religious movement that logically aims at making Rome its partner, it is well to explore why Paul and the apostles are so effective in the quest as described in Acts.

---

1. This supports the site of our dive that I described in this book's *Foreword*. What the Malta map notes as St. Paul's Bay has a wide, not rocky, mouth.

Paul's first attribute is his ability to convincingly teach an appealing gospel. He teaches Christ crucified and resurrected by God. This shows the power of God, giving credence to the promise of salvation and an afterlife in heaven. It also indicates that God's power by raising Jesus is greater than that of Rome, which tried to kill Jesus but could not keep him dead. Paul's gospel presents, therefore, a loving God, who wants people to love one another. Paul freely gives advice on morality and customs that he thinks is compatible with the faith. Faith gives instructions and comfort as well as promise. Existing in a community in love is a very attractive prospect. As noted previously, the contrast with the Roman political-religious culture is stark. The Christian political-religious movement grows.

Paul's leadership is also authoritative for the individual churches. He gives sound advice on settling internal church disputes and on relations with Roman authorities. Paul's belief in the gospel is so strong that he is willing to suffer great tribulations for it. He works hard and does not waver. Paul's demonstrated ability to heal and even raise from the dead serves to confirm his connection to Jesus and God, thereby affirming that he is their legitimate spokesman. He is credentialed. Because he is not arrogant or boastful, Paul easily delegates authority to the locals, thereby empowering them, both men and women. This aids recruitment. He cares for them, which they overwhelmingly acknowledge. He is on their side in opening a better life for them. In short, he lives and works for others.

The Christian political-religious movement grows.

Paul is also a very good manager of the entire Christian movement. He and the other apostles bring news of other churches soon to spread throughout the Roman Empire. Members of every political movement need to know that others are part of the same enterprise—that they are not alone. And if others believe in it, there must be truth and justice to it. Paul is an excellent networker. In the Roman world, letter writing is the mass media—the central vehicle for news and thought. Paul wisely employs it. He knows that his letters will be copied and passed around. The church is on the march. Every member is important, valued, and equal in God's love, whether man or woman, free or slave, or Jew or Gentile.

The Christian political-religious movement grows.

Paul's letters, the first Christian theology that we have, precedes the Gospels by decades. They illustrate the interconnectedness of the Empire in terms of travel, language, and messaging.

I will analyze the letters for clues as to the appeal and spread of Christianity. The movement is clearly subversive politically to the Roman state. By denigrating the Roman gods, Christianity, in effect, denigrates the rulers who rely on these gods to foster obedience and identity. This makes public displays of the new religion politically unwise. Although such displays are to be avoided, sometimes sufficient care is not taken. Paul and other apostles eventually pay the price.

Historians have established that the First Letter of Paul to the Thessalonians is the first letter still extant that he writes. That letter is followed by First Corinthians, Philippians, Galatians, Second Letter to the Corinthians, and finally Romans. Evidence of Paul's teaching the gospel, his leadership, and his management of the political-religious movement is all there.

I will first present his teaching of the Christian gospel and morality, then his church leadership, and finally his management of the movement.

Writing on behalf of Silvanus and Timothy, who, along with Paul, had previously visited the church of the Thessalonians, Paul praises them for their belief in the gospel that "came to you not only in word, but also in power and in the Holy Spirit and with full conviction." He notes that they have become "an example to all the believers in Macedonia and Achaia . . . your faith in God has gone forth everywhere . . . " (1 Thess 1:4–8). By doing so, Paul lets them know that they are part of a growing and thriving movement as a result of their outreach.

Beseeching them how they ought to live, Paul advises "that no man transgress" in lust "or wrong his brother . . . for you yourselves have been taught by God to love one another; and indeed you do love all the brethren throughout Macedonia" (1 Thess 4:8–10). The apocalypse is coming, Paul asserts. "But you are not in darkness, stay sober and put on the breastplate of faith and love, and for a helmet the hope of salvation. For God has not destined us for wrath, but to obtain salvation through our Lord Jesus Christ, who died for us so that whether we wake or sleep we might live with him. Therefore encourage one another and build on another up, just as you are doing" (1 Thess 4:13-18, 5:1-11).

Paul praises them. "For you are our glory and joy" (1 Thess 2:20) and thanks them for their hospitality. His leadership confirms that working through others works.

In his first letter to the Corinthians, Paul focuses on the gospel and how to live it. He first gives thanks to God for them "because of the grace of God which was given to you in Christ Jesus . . . so that you are not lacking in any spiritual gift . . . " (1 Cor 1:4-7). Then he deals with their internal conflicts. He wants "no dissension among you" on whom to follow, whether "Paul, Apollos, or Cephas . . . we preach Christ crucified" and all are workers for God (1 Cor 1:10-23). Paul teaches the gospel, focusing on the promise of the resurrection. "Now if Christ is preached as raised from the dead, how can some of you say that there is no resurrection of the dead? But if there is no resurrection of the dead, the Christ has not been raised; if Christ has not been raised, then our preaching is in vain and your faith is in vain" (1 Cor 15:12-14). The righteous will be raised, he writes.

Paul gives advice freely on sex, marriage, law-breaking, and diet. One piece of advice has political impact. Paul pleads that they not take church disputes to the authorities, who are unbelievers. In other letters, he puts this advice in the context of building the movement as unimpeded as possible by the Roman authorities. The more Christians enter the public arena, the more they will reveal their subversive nature and thus be repressed. Paul wants them to have unity, harmony, proper behavior, and love among themselves. He famously extols love: "Love is patient and kind; love is not jealous or boastful; it is not arrogant or rue. Love does not insist on its own way; it is not irritable or resentful; it does not rejoice at wrong, but rejoices in the right. Love bears all things, believes all things, hopes all things, endures all things" (1 Cor 13:4–7).

Paul writes to the Philippians, saying that he is . . . "thankful for your partnership in the gospel from the first day until now" (Phil 1:5), noting that they are "partakers with me of grace, both in my imprisonment and in the defense and confirmation of the gospel" (Phil 1:7). There is rejoicing in his faith and deliverance from imprisonment; he notes that even if not so fortunate to be free he will still honor his faith. Paul wants "to hear of you that you stand firm in one spirit, with one mind striving side by side for the faith of the gospel, and not frightened in anything by your opponents. This is a clear omen to them of their destruction, but of your salvation, and that from God" (Phil 1:27–28). Further affirmation of the gospel follows.

His letter to the Galatians, in comparison to those to the Corinthians and Romans, is short. Paul berates them for "deserting him who called you in Grace and turning to a different gospel—not that there is another gospel, but there are some who trouble you and want to pervert the gospel of Christ . . . let him be accursed" (Gal 1:6–9). With Cephas [Peter] in mind, Paul emphasizes that "a man is not justified by works of the law but through faith in Christ Jesus . . . " (Gal 2:16). He also finds no advantage in circumcision of the Gentiles. In this regard, he injects some sardonic humor, writing, "I wish those who unsettle you would mutilate themselves!" (Gal 5:12). Castigating the desires of the flesh, which he lists (and thereby apparently provokes some dispute), Paul writes that "the whole law is fulfilled in one word. 'You shall love your neighbor as yourself.'" Unity is stressed: "If we live by the Spirit, let us also walk by the Spirit. Let us have no self-conceit, no provoking of one another, no envy of one another" (Gal 5:25–26).

Paul continues to press the gospel in every letter. In his second to the Corinthians, he notes that in his first letter, upbraiding them for the dissension among themselves gave him pain. Now more positive, Paul repeats the gospel and salvation message. "I have confidence in you. I have great pride in you. I am filled with comfort" (2 Cor 7:4).

Part II—The Christian Bible

His letter to the Romans is almost entirely about the gospel and proper Christian behavior. Paul has not been to Rome, but intends to stop there on his way to Spain. On the face of it, his letter is designed to convince the Romans that he knows what he is talking and writing about. It is an introduction of himself and proof of his legitimacy as an apostle.

He gives his credentials right away, stating,

> Paul, a servant of Jesus Christ, called to be an apostle, set apart for the gospel of God, which he promised beforehand through his prophets in the holy scriptures, the gospel concerning his Son, who was descended from David according to the flesh, and designated Son of God in power according to the Spirit of holiness by his resurrection from the dead, Jesus Christ our Lord through whom we have received grace and apostleship to bring about obedience to the faith for the sake of his name among all nations, including yourselves who are called to belong to Jesus Christ. (Rom 1:1-6)

Through the rest of the first chapter, Paul thanks the Romans for their faith, repeats his own faith, and castigates the ungodly and wicked—those who reject God, have abnormal sex, and practice a long list of wicked behavior.

Concluding a long section of his letter on the topics of faith over law and works, that circumcision is unnecessary, and that God is also for the Gentiles, Paul concludes: "Therefore, since we are justified by faith, we have peace with God through our Lord Jesus Christ" (Rom 2, 3, 4, 5:1). Key phrases follow. "Christ died for us" (Rom 5:8); "eternal life through Jesus Christ our Lord" (Rom 5:21).

After reminding the Roman church that some of its members had committed sins of the flesh, Paul makes a sarcastic comment. "But thanks be to God, that you who were once slave to sin have become obedient from the heart to the standard of teaching to which you were committed, and, having been set free from sin, have become slaves to righteousness. I am speaking in human terms, because of your natural limitations" (Rom 6:17–19). One could wonder how this statement plays in Rome!

Some remarks from Paul unquestionably support the theme of this book—namely, that the political failure of Judea leads to the creation of the Gentile conversion and political movement that is designed to capture Rome. In addition, Paul believes that the Christian movement will redeem the Jews. Chapter 11 of Romans deals with the Jews.

> I ask, then, has God rejected his people? By no means! I myself am an Israelite, a descendant of Abraham, a member of the tribe of Benjamin. God has not rejected his people who he foreknew . . . So too at the present time there is a remnant, chosen by grace . . . What then? Israel has failed to obtain what it sought. The elect obtained it, but the rest were hardened . . . So I ask, have they stumbled so as to fall? By no means! But through their trespass salvation has come to the Gentiles, so as to make Israel jealous. Now if their trespass means riches for the world, and if their failure means riches for the Gentiles, how much more will their full inclusion mean. (Rom 11:1–12)

Perhaps I am misreading Paul, but, besides noting that Christianity is rooted in Jewish failure, he seems to suggest that the salvation of the Jews will come from Christians.

Finally, Paul's commentary on the gospel and proper behavior concludes with a political admonition that we have noted previously. It is a long passage and an important one, especially to Roman Christians living in the very capital of the Empire. Here, in a nutshell, is the strategy for swelling the Christian movement—relatively unimpeded by the authorities and, at the same time, increasingly attractive to the people and eventually to the ruling elite. It is absolutely brilliant political advice!

> Let love be genuine; hate what is evil, hold fast to what is good; love one another with brotherly affection; outdo one another in showing honor. Never flag in zeal, be aglow with the Spirit, serve the Lord. Rejoice in your

Part II—The Christian Bible

hope, be patient in tribulation, be constant in prayer. Contribute to the needs of the saints, practice hospitality.

Bless those who persecute you; bless and do not curse them. Rejoice with those who rejoice, weep with those who weep. Live in harmony with one another; do not be haughty, but associate with the lowly, never be conceited. Repay no one evil for evil, but take thought for what is noble in the sight of all. If possible, so far as it depends upon you, live peaceably with all. Beloved, never avenge yourselves, but leave it to the wrath of God; for it is written 'Vengeance is mine. I will repay, says the Lord.' No, 'if your enemy is hungry, feed him; if he is thirsty, give him, drink; for by so doing you will heap burning coals upon his head.' Do not be overcome by evil, but overcome evil with good.

Let every person be subject to the governing authorities. For there is no authority except from God, and those that exist have been instituted by God. Therefore he who resists the authorities resist what God has appointed, and those who resist will incur judgment. For rulers are not a terror to good conduct, but to bad. Would you have no fear of him who is in authority? Then do what is good, and you will receive his approval, for he is God's servant for your good. But if you do wrong, be afraid, for he does not bear the sword in vain; he is the servant of God to execute his wrath on the wrongdoer. Therefore one must be subject, not only to avoid God's wrath but also for the sake of conscience. For the same reason you also pay taxes, for the authorities are ministers of God, attending to this very thing. Pay all of them their dues, taxes to whom taxes are due, revenue to whom revenue is due, respect to whom respect is due, honor to whom honor is due.

Owe no one anything, except to love one another; for he who loves his neighbor has fulfilled the law. The commandments, 'You shall not commit adultery, You shall not kill, You shall not steal, You shall not covet' and any other commandment, are summed up in this sentence, 'You shall love your neighbor as yourself.' Love does no wrong to a neighbor; therefore love is the fulfilling of the law. (Rom 12:14–21, 13:1–10)

The political message to the Roman church could not be clearer.

By being loving and good, especially in Rome, you will not provoke popular opinion or Roman authorities to oppose the movement. If anything, such a lifestyle will have great appeal to non-Christians—potential converts—who want a better life. The movement will expand.

By blessing those who persecute you as subversives, not repaying evil for evil, and living peaceably with all, you will not incite and swell opposition that will stifle the movement.

By treating Gentile opponents well, helping them overcome hunger and thirst, you will present a sharp contrast between your goodness and their badness. This will reduce hostility to the movement, which needs time to grow.

By being obedient to the Roman authorities, obeying their laws, and paying taxes, you will not suffer their sword. Instead, you will appear as model citizens worthy of emulation. In addition, you will avoid political battles in which you are bound to lose. These could even result in crushing the movement.

By loving your Gentile neighbor, you will be in an advantageous position to recruit them to a movement on the move.

While Paul's political strategy is not carried out perfectly—there are severe persecutions and setbacks—it is sufficiently adhered to. It works.

Paul's effective leadership style is also revealed in his letters and has many facets.

Focusing on creating and supporting Christian churches in cities throughout the Roman Empire recognizes that Rome is an urban civilization. That is where important events originate and where political power—his ultimate aim—lies.

Giving praise and thanks to the churches, evident in all his letters except First Corinthians, but later corrected in his second letter to them, gives them an important approbation from one of the most prominent apostles. They are on track establishing the

Part II—The Christian Bible

Christian movement. Knowing that it is succeeding in its mission motivates every organization to continue that mission.

Arming the churches with the gospel—the same gospel to all—serves to unify the movement and prevent theological disputes among them. A movement too concerned with itself and not its outward mission all too often fails.

Working to help resolve their internal problems, Paul seeks to have the churches—as he has done with those in Corinth, Galatia, and Rome—focus on unity, gearing up for the principal recruiting mission for the movement.

Rejecting a title and a formal position designed to rule the churches allows the local leadership to have authority and responsibility for growing the movement. Paul appears to the churches as their servant and helper, not their master.

Collecting and providing aid (funds) to the needy church in Jerusalem—as noted in First Corinthians, Galatians, and Romans—illustrates two aspects of effective leadership. Every politician knows that those who contribute to political campaigns are, in effect, investing in the candidate, committing to the candidate, and becoming active on the candidate's side, and contributing creates loyalty. Secondly, providing necessary funds to a needy organization also strengthens the candidate's organization. Therefore, raising and contributing money serves the movement.

Finally, as noted before, informing the churches of the activities of other churches, connecting other apostles with a network of churches, and showing that the movement is on the move throughout the Empire has the beneficial effect of confirming the rightness and great potential of the movement. Paul's letters always include news from other churches and the apostles working among them.

- In Thessalonians, Paul mentions Silvanus and Timothy.
- He praises Apollos, Cephas, and Timothy in First Corinthians; says that he has heard from Chloe about their quarrels; and gives news about the churches in Jerusalem and Asia.
- In Philippians, Paul notes his conversion of Roman soldiers during his imprisonment; praises women apostles Euodia

and Syntyche, who labor in the gospel; and informs them about the travels of Timothy and Epaphroditus.

- He gives news in Galatians about being in Jerusalem with Cephas [Peter] and the Lord's brother James and later there with Barnabas and Titus, and with Cephas in Antioch.

- In Second Corinthians, Paul informs the church there about the good work of the churches in Macedonia and tells them to expect a visit from Titus.

- In Romans, he tells of his intention to go to Spain and Jerusalem with aid from Corinth and Macedonia; commends sister Phoebe, a helper; and asks them to greet Prisca, Aquila, Epaenetus, Mary, Andronicus, and many others.

Before the Internet there is Paul.

── CHAPTER 9 ──

The Politics of Death and Resurrection

IN CHAPTERS 7 AND 8, I emphasize that the promise of resurrection—eternal life—becomes a great selling point for building the Christian movement. Further thoughts on this topic lead me to believe that there are additional political functions.

Besides Jesus' triumph over Rome, his resurrection overcomes a primal fear of one's extinction. When one's childhood is long gone and health problems intrude into daily life, death becomes an ever present near probability, then certainty, in one's line of thought. A case can be made that the inevitability of death is *a*, if not *the*, mother of religion.

Eternal life with God in Heaven is not prominent in Judaism. Although the Pharisees, under the sway of Greek thought, did hold this belief, it is one that, in my reading of the Hebrew Bible, plays a small role in their devotion to God. The old joke, with its obvious Christian bias, that the Sadducees were "sad-you-see," results from their non-belief in eternal life. Jewish devotion to God, itself, dominates their belief system. Their reward for their fealty is God's protection and comfort in this life. "The Lord is my shepherd, I shall not want . . . " from the Twenty-Third Psalm exemplifies this pillar of faith. The emphasis on a good and fulfilling life results from adherence to God's laws. Yet, and I am on thin ice here, the

The Politics of Death and Resurrection

Talmud (an authoritative body of Jewish traditions) refers to Olam Ha-Ba, the World to Come, which indicates that something exists beyond death.

In contrast, the Christian Bible's elevation of human resurrection, whether body or soul, dominates the canon and proves to be an essential promise to create Christians and serves as a unifier of the faith. Jesus, Paul, and the Apostles rarely fail to proclaim it.

The promise of resurrection or an afterlife also has other political functions besides recruitment for the religious-political movement.

It cements devotion to Jesus, the one who makes the promise and whose own resurrection proves it. There should be no surprise that the agent of God—the person passing along the potent belief—is revered and worshipped as part of the Trinity of Father, Son, and Holy Spirit. As the messiah, Jesus' teachings provide the foundation of Christian religious practice, although departures from it punctuate the history of the church from its very foundation as established by Paul and the apostles.

The promise of resurrection, once Christians believe it, softens the blow of persecution and even causes some to welcome that suffering. Didn't Jesus and many of his apostles suffer persecution? Bearing it, following Christ's example in one's own life, means that one is emulating Jesus. To those who say that dying for one's faith cheapens life, early Christians would say that such an outcome validates a true Christian life and produces an even better one. Steadfastness results. In the difficult but necessary decades and centuries for the Christian movement to grow and eventually be grafted onto the Roman Empire, this overall solid adherence to the faith preserves and grows the church. In addition, standing up for the faith by enduring persecution cannot help but convince potential Christians of that faith's validity.

In later church-state history (and in Islam), heaven has been used to build patriotism for fighting wars. Dead warriors are honored, with priests, imams, and modern chaplains providing comfort to the families of the departed while championing their sacrifice and preaching their place in heaven. "Onward, Christian soldiers, Marching as to war . . . " Christian history relates that one of the motives of Constantine for his conversion and setting the stage for making Christianity Rome's official religion is to have God and Christians on his side in an upcoming battle. A single God also helps unify Rome's religious culture, which, under traditional Roman gods, had only fractured and failed to inspire the Empire's masses. Politics over the centuries has made the ruling class patricians pay more attention to the plebeians, who have become essential for mobilizing Rome for war.

For social stability and to keep the masses in line, the widespread belief in the afterlife helps makes it easier for rulers to govern. Laws are connected to their Judeo-Christian roots—especially the Ten Commandments and the sayings of Jesus. Avoiding Hell feeds good behavior and obedience to those who command the religion. All this is predicated on the theme that I strongly emphasize throughout my analysis: that politics and religion are partners in biblical times and for centuries thereafter. Even the separation of church and state, as many countries now practice, hardly sullies their mutual devotion, for which the United States is the foremost example.

Finally, even funerals (Christian or otherwise) invariably celebrate the contributions of the deceased to other people and to society. This bolsters patriotism.

— CHAPTER 10 —

Epilogue: Unanswered Questions

How did Abraham, Moses, Joshua, Samuel, and other Hebrew leaders feel and react to being ordered around by God?

There is not much commentary from these leaders about their fealty to God, perhaps because he is so real to them, so communicative to them, and so helpful. They believe.

The evidence that we have provides a solid elaboration on this answer.

All these leaders act in a way which indicates that they feel honored to be chosen by God as his instrument to attain Godly goals. Even initial reluctance by Moses to do God's bidding quickly fades. He, like the others, must believe that God made a good choice in them and accept his orders. They all express their inadequacy in making their own decisions, fearful that they cannot perform successfully on their own. Proof of this is the many instances that they ask God the "What if" question. "What if," asks Moses, "Pharaoh ignores my demands to let my people go?" (Exod 6:12) "What if," Abraham asks God, "I do not know how to possess the land you promise" (Gen 15:8). They need answers. This leads to a very human motive for obeying God. The leaders must be relieved that God is taking responsibility for the outcome of the orders. By telling the people that God will deliver them, the burden of proof rests with God, not them. God is the chief politician and theologian. Perhaps they harbor the idea that someday they will have the knowledge and experience to make their own decisions, asserting themselves and escaping from heavy subordination. There is not much evidence for this before Joshua, and even he remains largely obedient. Later rulers, as we note, are less so.

Do the Bibles indicate that God is losing command of political history?

The answer is yes, and this answer should be expected.

Early humans in the Hebrew Bible—Adam, Eve, Abraham, and even Moses—have very little knowledge about anything. They have little historical experience, few sources of instruction, and little means of employing any type of science. God, therefore, has the opportunity, even the necessity, to instruct them. And human ignorance creates the necessity to listen to God and obey. In addition, God is portrayed as having a set agenda—from creating a nation, picking leaders, establishing a homeland, leaving bondage, establishing laws, and crossing Jordan, to conquering the Promised Land. The fact that these actions are agreeable to the Hebrews also makes them listen and obey.

Then we witness Moses and Joshua disobeying, David blatantly sinning, and Solomon, at times not even listening to God. A vast increase in knowledge and self-confidence in one's own judgment, thus taking advantage of free will, produces increasingly human-directed political behavior. Israelite leaders believe that they have less need to listen to God. Reluctantly, God appears to accept that he is losing control. He tells Moses that an angel, not he, will lead the Israelites across the Jordan, and tells Samuel that he regrets allowing the Israelites to have a king replace him.

This increase in knowledge and self-confidence also brings the common people into play politically. They develop expectations that their leaders often have to accede to. The voice of the people may not be the voice of God, but it plays an increasingly important role, slowly competing with other sources of behavior.

Lastly, ambition, the love of power, and the concentration of power in singular hands turns leaders into what they think is the ability to make history according to their own choosing. Those

Epilogue: Unanswered Questions

who follow Solomon increasingly exhibit this trait. As the prophets say, they turn away from God and his laws.

The Christian Bible continues this trend. God is portrayed as playing key roles in the birth of Jesus, his survival under threat by Herod, and his baptism by John. Thereafter, Jesus and his disciples take charge. In fact, they have to. Jesus cannot be the messiah, the Son of God, if he is only a messenger of God; he has to be the one calling the shots. Even before his crucifixion, Jesus petitions God to change the story line, but God does not intervene.

Just as significant, Christians believe that it is the obligation of most humans to seek God and to listen to and follow his word. Faith is a choice. This is a further indication that humans have the prime responsibility for their behavior, good or bad. Modern society is founded on this fundamental belief, whether it pertains to political, criminal, ethical, scientific, or any other type of behavior. Pleas that "the devil made me do it" or that "God told me to do it" carry no weight for wrongdoing. In fact, they are phrases used as jokes by stand-up comedians.

Is everything in the Hebrew and Christian Bibles God's plan?

This is not the same question that was answered above. The fact that God is increasingly not in charge does not mean that events are not part of his plan. It is not farfetched to believe that God accepts and welcomes the further empowerment of humans by humans. This could very well be part of God's plan.

And it is close to inevitable when reading both Bibles not to conclude that its political course is definitely following God's plan. The entire Hebrew Bible reflects it. Even if the Christian Bible mutes God's politics, Jesus' efforts to lay the foundation for a political-religious movement that will subvert Rome is portrayed as being what God wants. There is no separation between God and Jesus on the fundamental political course, as it is described in both the gospels and letters.

But it does raise some very important questions. Are the Jews still God's chosen people?

To the question "Has God rejected his chosen people?" Paul answers, "By no means!" (Rom 11:1).

Part II—The Christian Bible

First, what motive would God have for abandoning the Jews as his chosen people? There are none that make any sense. To argue that the Jews brought on the demise of their sovereign Judea by the Romans, or that some of their leaders called for the crucifixion of Jesus does not mean that God is responsible for such failures. Being chosen does not mean or require that they be empowered to be perfect. The Jews take on increasing responsibility and political power of their own choosing. The mistakes are theirs.

To argue that the Inquisition, pogroms, and even the Holocaust are results of God's abandonment also makes no sense. Simply put, non-Jews are to blame for these misfortunes. Nothing that the Jews have done, or that we have even imagined them having done, provide any legitimate rationale whatever for their gross mistreatment. Some very wicked political leaders have used their persecution of Jews for their own purposes. The most obvious example is Hitler, using his "final solution" to create what he considered to be the purification of the Aryan German race—a condition that he believed would strengthen Germany in order to conquer others. Just being Jews made them targets of persecution.

And the belief among Jews that they are still God's chosen people helps them endure and survive, often quite well. They care and support one another.

The Jews have had a profound effect on world history and politics. The failed Jewish revolt of 66–70 CE and the one that follows it—nothing seems to have been learned in Jerusalem about politics—creates, or rather inflates, the Jewish diaspora. Here the Jews perform a great service to the world. More than any other peoples, they enrich what has become the world's dominant culture. Monotheistic as well as poetically, ethically, musically, economically, historically, architecturally, and artistically advanced, this cultural contribution by the Jews has no equal. And it serves to civilize politics. The impact of the Ten Commandments on civil law, morality, and ethics has reshaped human behavior.

In short, Jews believe that they are God's chosen and act accordingly. This belief is the cement of historical Jewish unity; it supports their great cultural mission and drives the impulse to

Epilogue: Unanswered Questions

return to the Promised Land. Additionally, orthodox Christianity and Islam accept Jews as people of the book, the same God for all, and consider Jews to be a true expression of his will.

Jesus lives, dies, and is resurrected as a Jew. He has no other religion. Jesus is a member of the chosen people. His aim, as I have argued, consists of expanding God's people, bringing God to the entire world. Logically, that world is charged to protect his chosen. That role, as we know, has been seriously flawed.

What is the evidence that Christians are charged to protect the Jews, God's first chosen?

Here is the first quote from Paul in his letter to the Romans (noted above) regarding whether the Jews are still God's chosen (Rom 11:1-2, 29-32):

> I ask then, has God rejected his people? By no means! I myself am an Israelite, a descendant of Abraham, a member of the tribe of Benjamin. God has not rejected his people who he foreknew ... For the gifts and the calling of God are irrevocable. Just as you were once disobedient to God but have now received mercy because of their disobedience, so they have now been disobedient to God but have now received mercy because of their disobedience, so they have been disobedient in order that, by the mercy shown to you, they too may now receive mercy. For God has imprisoned all in the disobedience so that he may be merciful to all.

More importantly, Jesus is presented in the Christian Bible as the King of the Jews and is treated on that self-image by Pilate, a title that Jesus never renounces. Logically, Jesus expects that his followers, both in the religious-political movement that he establishes and its eventual merging with real political power, would take his people under their wing.

Paul's charge and Jesus' expectation that Christians are obliged to protect the Jews, although often badly neglected throughout Christian history, are now more evident.

Christians, it should be noted, also play a key role in the re-establishment of modern Israel. Ironically, their persecution of the

Part II—The Christian Bible

Jews creates, for Jews, the motive and the will to re-establish it. And Christian support for the Jews' return to the Promised Land rests on the need for Christian forgiveness and the continuing recognition that the Jews—still a chosen people—need a homeland. However checkered, the Jews receive support for transport to Palestine, obtain military training by the British in World War II (50,000 future Israelis serve in the war), receive arms from Czechoslovakia for their independence fight, and receive strong diplomatic support from the United States and the UN.

Does my political analysis of the Bible provide information that explains why there are ferocious religious wars in more recent history?

The answer is yes, although I am not the first to trace the connection. For that, I am indebted to John M. Owen IV, the Ambassador J. Taylor and Mrs. Marion R. Taylor Professor of Politics at the University of Virginia. In his journal essay (adopted from his book *Confronting Political Islam: Six Lessons from the West's Past*), Owen brilliantly makes the case that the religious wars in seventeenth century Europe provide the template for understanding the religious wars that rack the Middle East today. They have the same pattern.[1]

I will take his thesis and put it in the context of my work here, borrowing heavily from it.

I argue that the union of religion and state is fundamental to understanding Hebrew history and the Christian movement to capture a protective and faithful state. In late Medieval Europe, the Roman Catholic Church serves as the official religion of many states. Interests of state, represented by autocratic rulers, soon lead these rulers to challenge the political influence of the Roman Catholic Church and their states' connection to it. Catholic states fight back. England's Henry VIII is only one of a number of Protestant monarchs to fight, in effect, for the separation of his state from official Christianity. The Catholic Church, in response, then mobilizes its loyal states, fighting desperately to restore the

---

1. Owen IV, "From Calvin to the Caliphate: What Europe's Wars of Religion Tell Us About the Modern Middle East," 77–89.

Epilogue: Unanswered Questions

universal union of church and state. Religious conflicts rack the German principalities, France, and the Dutch Republic; they fade, only to be reignited by a Protestant revolt in Bohemia. The Thirty Years' War, from 1618 to 1648, finds various rulers in Northern Europe wanting more control, and that means having a state religion under their hegemony. The 1648 Treaty of Westphalia ends the horrific Religious Wars, with Protestant and Catholic rulers free to create or maintain their state religions. In both kinds of states, church power over the centuries fades, leaving secular authorities in firmer control.

Owen traces the growth of secularism in the Middle East, in part from modernist rulers such as Ataturk in Turkey, but largely from European secular imperialism. And this separation of religion and state is anathema for the Islamic Jihadists. These events almost immediately provoke Islamists to organize resistance movements. Their first spectacular success happens in Iran with the 1979 Islamic Revolution, which overthrows the secular shah, who is also an ally of the increasingly interventionist United States. Washington's frequent meddling and combat in the Middle East helps trigger further resistance by Islamists, as does the Soviet intervention in Afghanistan. The Taliban, the al Qaeda movement, and ISIS now engage in a militant jihad in order to restore the union of Islam with political authority. The United States and its "puppets" are the targets.

The church-state issue is far from dead. In a different context, the Jewish state of Israel, after years of war with its Muslim neighbors, conducts a decade-long struggle with the half-Islamist, half-secular Palestinians.

The re-establishment of Israel and the course of its development lead to the following question for today: Do the Bibles have any relevance, any lessons, to help us understand the current Arab-Israeli conflict?

The re-establishment of Israel cannot be imagined without recollecting the story of the land promised to the Israelites in the Hebrew Bible. Jewish political history demands that they look to Zion, contemplate their Holy Land, and, whether yearning to live there or not, at least celebrate it and give it their support.

Part II—The Christian Bible

Most Western Christians reflecting on their Old Testament—one that they read and believe that God has given to his Chosen People—also exhibit a spiritual attachment to the Jewish state. Nothing about its rebirth seems strange to them. Their religious roots are Jewish. The crime that their savior died for—being King of the Jews—also cements the Christian attachment to Israel.

Both Bibles include the understandable expectation that the non-Jews living in the former Roman Palestine will cause trouble. They live there, too, and will not be favored. The fight over the control of land should come as no surprise to the Bible reader.

The issue of political power is more complex.

Political conditions in Roman Judea noted at the end of the Hebrew Bible and all through the Christian book have Jews under occupation and defeat. Rome is the master.

Today, the Jews are the master and occupier. Like Rome, they are militarily without equal in the entire Middle East. They are nuclear armed, have the world's fourth largest army, and are as technologically advanced as any military. In addition, Israel has the loyal backing of the United States. Israel can defeat and lay waste any foe. Opponents, whether Hezbollah in Lebanon or Hamas in Gaza, are forced to employ guerrilla tactics, terrorism, and crude offensive weapons, such as primitive rockets. They are weak and vastly inferior to Israel. Even Iran—Israel's current designated "existential threat"—lacks nuclear weapons and is unlikely to get them or even seek them.

The constant occasion of war in both Bibles is repeated in modern times in the Middle East. Israel, since its 1948 Independence War, has been at war for more years than it has been at peace, having fought at least ten wars in sixty-seven years.

The Palestinians are like the Jews under Rome. Their plight—not free, embargoed, blockaded, incarcerated at whim, denied travel rights, and effectively alone politically—compels periodic, seemingly irrational, violent thrusts at the occupiers. They, like the ancient Jews, believe that God is on their side. The Palestinians also act knowing that they will pay the higher price. Still, like the occupied Jews under Rome before them, they do it.

Epilogue: Unanswered Questions

Military action appears the default strategy of both sides.

If the Bible hints at the Palestinians' ultimate fate, it would be their forced removal from a greater Israel, enlarging an already existing diaspora. The Palestinians, like the Jews in their diaspora, enrich foreign cultures with their love of learning, poetry, endurance, and good works. But also like the Jewish diaspora, the Palestinians suffer persecution, discrimination, and political foul play.

However, a number of my Israeli acquaintances and the official United States policy prefer that a Palestinian state be established. They envision a far different outcome than the present course. Rather than eliminating or expelling Palestinians—as God demanded that the Israelites do to the Canaanites under Joshua—the same separation effect can be accomplished by giving them a state. They make the case that the two states would be natural allies, an economic powerhouse, and a sea of tranquility in an arena of tempest. And as former Israeli Prime Minister Ehud Barak told me at a reception at the World Economic Forum in Davos, Switzerland, a Palestinian state will keep Israel both Jewish and Democratic. By this he means that keeping the Palestinians within a greater Israel, soon to outnumber the Jews, and making them democratic citizens with the vote will finish Israel as a Jewish state, whereas denying them the vote will end democracy.

Alas, as long as control of the biblical land is paramount, getting to a Palestinian state looms close to impossible. With force as the default posture for both sides, trust nowhere in evidence, and outside powers' meddling in the conflict making it more intractable, biblically based optimism wanes.

It will take God's intervention, similar to that in the beginning of the Hebrew Bible, to resolve the conflict. But he has left it to humans to act. As Paul and modern theologians note, God's grace does not depend upon correct human behavior. Although Jews, Christians, and Muslims have done some very bad things, they are still, according to the Bible and Quran, God's chosen. They are instructed to abide by the Ten Commandments and the Golden Rule.

These instructions are not God's hidden politics. They are on the marquee.

Bibliography

Aslan, Reza. *Zealot: The Life and Times of Jesus of Nazareth*. New York: Random House, 2013.

Ehrman, Bart D. *How Jesus Became God; The Exaltation of a Jewish Preacher from Galilee*. New York: Harper One, 2014.

Feiler, Bruce. *Walking the Bible: A Journey Through the Five Books of Moses*. New York: William Morrow, 2001.

Hawking, Stephen. *A Brief History of Time*. New York: Bantam Books, 1988.

Mead, Margaret. "Warfare is Only an Invention – Not a Biological Necessity." ASIA, XL (1940).

Owen IV, John M. *Confronting Political Islam: Six Lessons from the West's Past*. Princeton University Press, 2015.

———. "From Calvin to the Caliphate: What Europe's Wars of Religion Tell Us About the Modern Middle East." *Foreign Affairs* 94:3 (2015) 77–89.

von Clausewitz, Carl. *On War*. Princeton University Press, 1976.

Walzer, Michael. *In God's Shadow: Politics in the Hebrew Bible*. New Haven: Yale University Press, 2012.

X (Kennan, George F.). "The Sources of Soviet Conduct." *Foreign Affairs* 25:4 (1947) 566–82.

www.ingramcontent.com/pod-product-compliance
Lightning Source LLC
Chambersburg PA
CBHW072145160426
43197CB00012B/2259